Preschool-K-1
GIANT BASIC SKILLS™
Phonics & Spelling Workbook

Modern Publishing
A Division of Unisystems, Inc.
New York, New York 10022
Series UPC Number: 49610

Cover art by Suzanne Vasilak
Illustrated by Arthur Friedman
Educational Consultant, Shereen Gertel Rutman, M.S.

Copyright © 1998 by Modern Publishing,
a division of Unisystems, Inc.

™Giant Basic Skills III Preschool–K-1 Workbook is a trademark
of Modern Publishing, a division of Unisystems, Inc.

TO THE PARENTS

Dear Parents,

By using the Giant Basic Skills Preschool–K–1 Workbooks, you are helping your child build an important connection between home and school. These workbooks have been carefully designed by educators to teach children skills in a developmentally appropriate manner. The activities build on the growing abilities of your child. Each section begins with simple exercises, and the age level increases gradually as children practice and master various skills. With your guidance, children will enjoy working on the activities and gain important learning skills at the same time.

Following are some suggestions to help make your time together enjoyable and rewarding for your child.

- Work on this book when both you and your child are calm, relaxed, and not tired.

- Choose a quiet place to work together.

- Make sure you have the materials you need, such as pencils and crayons or markers.

- Encourage your child to work on activities appropriate to his or her skill level. Each section begins with preschool-level activities and progresses through kindergarten to first grade level.

- Talk about each page and make sure your child understands the directions.

- Work on a few pages at each sitting. Rather than do too much, find ways to extend the activities away from the book.

- Compliment your child's work. Praise will encourage your child to accomplish more.

- Have fun! The time spent working on this book should be enjoyable for you and your child.

ESSENTIAL SKILLS

The repetitive activities within each chapter have been designed to help children learn to sort, separate, put together, and figure out—the organizational skills so necessary for learning and thinking. Activities in each section progress from easiest to most challenging.

CHAPTER 1   Phonics Readiness
This chapter invites children to use skills that lay the groundwork for reading, such as **visual and auditory discrimination**, **noticing details (including similarities and differences)**, and **reproducing sounds**.

CHAPTER 2   Alphabet Skills
Children practice **letter recognition** and **letter concept skills** in this section. They **notice details** and use **visual discrimination** to **identify and match uppercase and lowercase letters**.

CHAPTER 3   Beginning Consonants
Sound/symbol association and **recognizing initial consonants** are explored in this chapter. Children practice **writing letters** and **drawing pictures** to extend their understanding of these concepts.

CHAPTER 4   More About Consonants
Exercises extend children's knowledge of **sound/symbol association**. They practice **recognizing medial and ending consonants, auditory discrimination skills**, and **following multiple directions**.

CHAPTER 5   Short Vowels
As children develop a better understanding of the **association between sounds, symbols, and words**, they are introduced to activities that focus on vowels. They use **auditory discrimination skills** to **compare sounds that are alike** and **recognize short vowel sounds**.

CHAPTER 6   Long Vowels
This chapter builds on children's knowledge of **sound/symbol association**. Matching activities help children to practice **auditory discrimination skills** and **recognize long vowel sounds**. Children also **identify long vowel sounds spelled in various ways** and practice **writing words**.

CHAPTER 7   Combining Consonants
Exercises emphasize how **consonants can be blended together**. Children's understanding of **sound/symbol relationships** helps them to recognize consonant blends. Children extend their knowledge of phonics by **identifying beginning and ending consonant digraphs**.

CHAPTER 8   Word Families
Basic knowledge of **rhyming words** and an understanding of the **association of sounds, symbols, and letters** helps children **identify word families**. Children also practice **forming new words**.

CHAPTER 9   Synonyms
This chapter focuses on **vocabulary development**. Children are introduced to synonyms and learn to **recognize synonyms in a group of words**.

CHAPTER 10   Antonyms
Exercises in this chapter develop children's understanding of opposites. As children **identify antonyms in a group of words**, they enhance their vocabulary.

CHAPTER 11   Homonyms
The practice pages in this section help children **identify and distinguish between homonyms**. New vocabulary is developed as children **recognize homonyms in a group of words**.

CHAPTER 12   Compound Words
This chapter gives children the opportunity to use their vocabulary skills to **identify and form compound words**. They also practice **using compound words in sentences**.

TABLE OF CONTENTS

PHONICS READINESS

Look at the pictures in each row.
Cross out the one that is different.
Color the others.

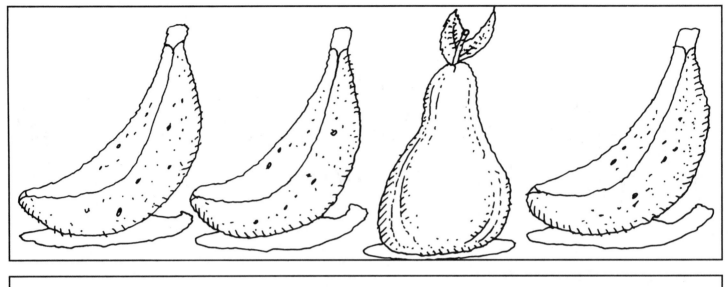

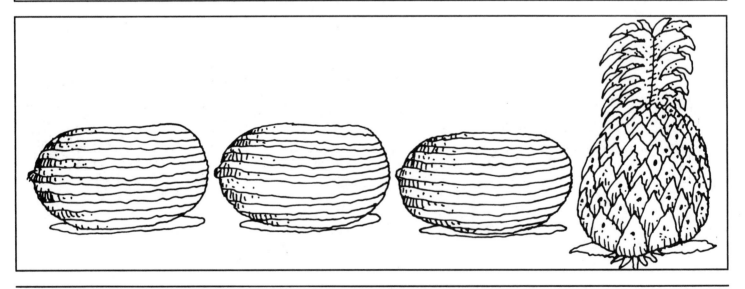

Skills: Visual discrimination; Noticing differences; Following directions

PHONICS READINESS

Look at the pictures in each row.
Cross out the one that is different.
Color the others.

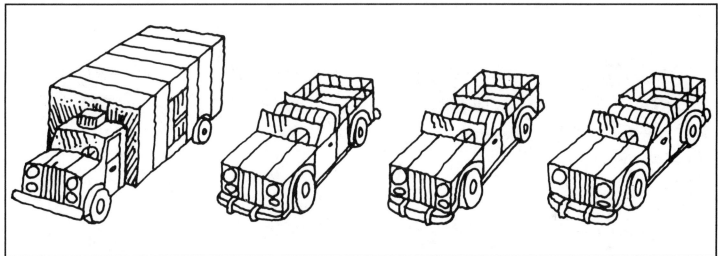

Skills: Visual discrimination; Noticing differences; Following directions

PHONICS READINESS

Look at the pictures in each row.
Cross out the one that is different.
Color the others.

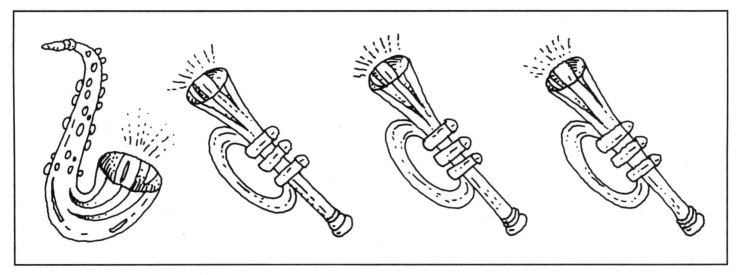

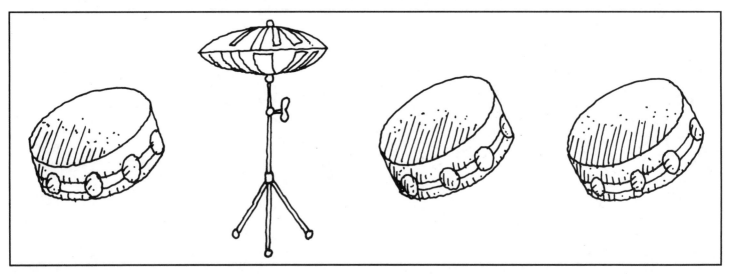

Skills: Visual discrimination; Noticing differences; Following directions

PHONICS READINESS

Look at the pictures in each row.
Cross out the one that is different.
Color the others.

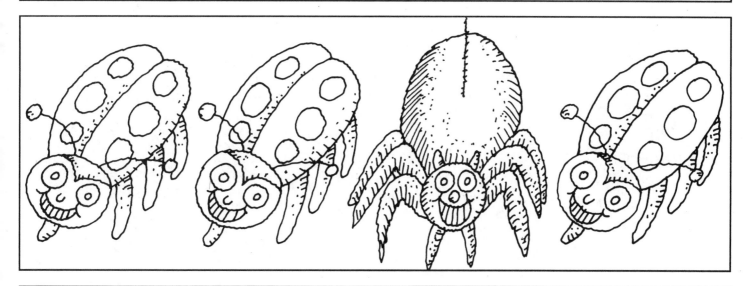

Skills: Visual discrimination; Noticing differences; Following directions

PHONICS READINESS

Look at the pictures on this page.
Find two of each picture.
Color each pair of pictures exactly the same way.

Skills: Visual discrimination; Noticing details; Following directions

PHONICS READINESS

Look at the pictures on this page.
Find two of each picture.
Color each pair of pictures exactly the same way.

Skills: Visual discrimination; Noticing details; Following directions

PHONICS READINESS

Look at the pictures on this page.
Find two of each picture.
Color each pair of pictures exactly the same way.

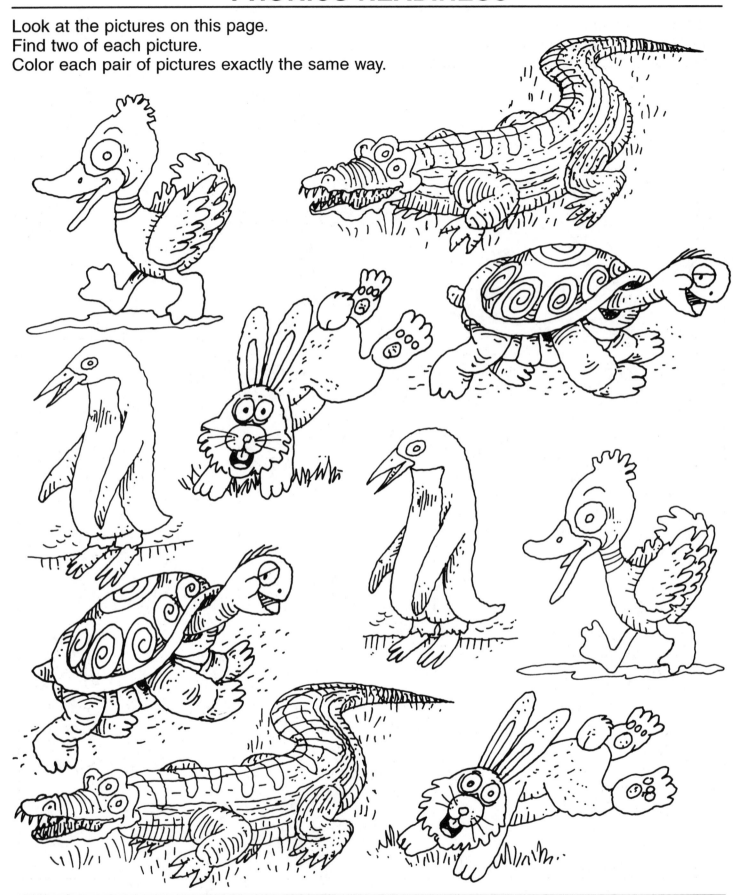

Skills: Visual discrimination; Noticing details; Following directions

PHONICS READINESS

Look at the pictures in each box.
Compare each pair of pictures and find what is missing.
Then draw what is missing in each picture.

Skills: Visual discrimination; Noticing details; Completing a picture; Following directions

PHONICS READINESS

Look at the pictures in each box.
Compare each pair of pictures and find what is missing.
Then draw what is missing in each picture.

Skills: Visual discrimination; Noticing details; Completing a picture; Following directions

PHONICS READINESS

Look at the first picture in each row and say its name.
Circle the picture whose name rhymes with it.

Skills: Auditory discrimination; Reproducing sounds

PHONICS READINESS

Look at the first picture in each row and say its name.
Circle the picture whose name rhymes with it.

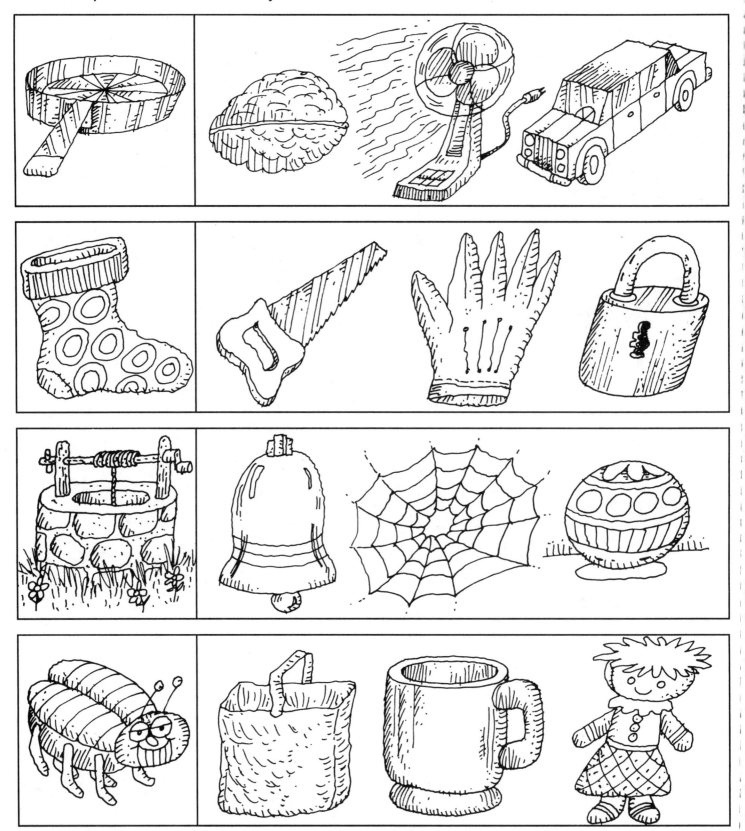

Skills: Auditory discrimination; Reproducing sounds

PHONICS READINESS

Look at the first picture in each row and say its name.
Circle the picture whose name rhymes with it.

Skills: Auditory discrimination; Reproducing sounds

PHONICS READINESS

Look at the first picture in each row and say its name.
Circle the picture whose name rhymes with it.

Skills: Auditory discrimination; Reproducing sounds

PHONICS READINESS

Look at the first picture in each row and say its name.
Circle the picture whose name rhymes with it.

Skills: Auditory discrimination; Reproducing sounds

PHONICS READINESS

Look at each picture and say its name.
Draw lines to match the rhyming pictures.

Skills: Auditory discrimination; Reproducing sounds

PHONICS READINESS

Look at each picture and say its name.
Draw lines to match the rhyming pictures.

Skills: Auditory discrimination; Reproducing sounds

PHONICS READINESS

Look at each picture and say its name.
Draw lines to match the rhyming pictures.

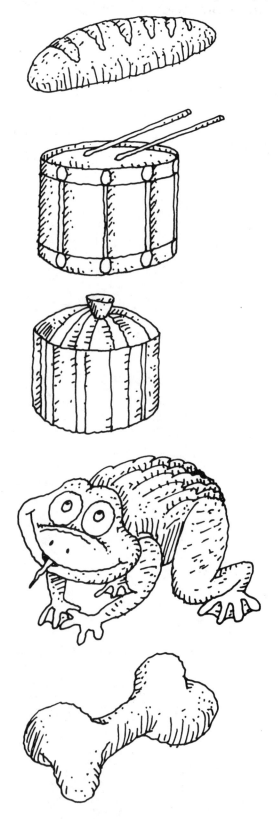

Skills: Auditory discrimination; Reproducing sounds

PHONICS READINESS

Look at each sock hanging out to dry.
Say the name of the picture on each sock.
Color the socks that have pictures whose names rhyme with the word **sock**.

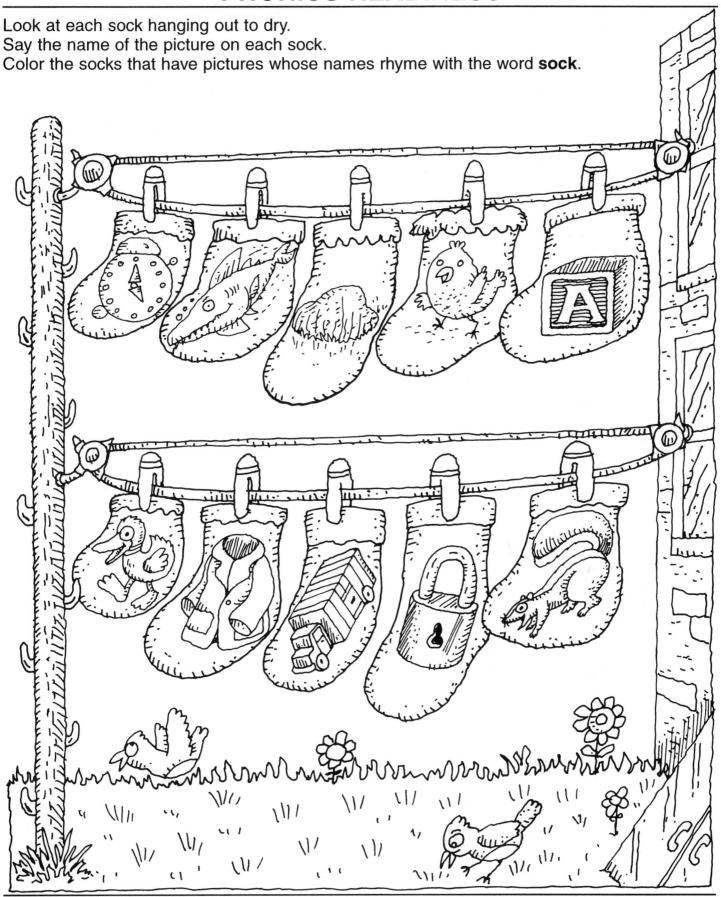

Skills: Auditory discrimination; Reproducing sounds

ALPHABET SKILLS

Look at the letters in each row.
Cross out the one that is different.
Circle the others.

Skills: Visual discrimination; Noticing details; Recognizing differences; Following directions

ALPHABET SKILLS

Look at the letters in each row.
Cross out the one that is different.
Circle the others.

g q g g g

v v v w v

s s z s s

n r n n n

Skills: Visual discrimination; Noticing details; Recognizing differences; Following directions

ALPHABET SKILLS

Look at the first letter in each row.
Look at the rest of the letters in each row.
Circle the ones that are exactly like the first letter.

b	q	b	p	b	b
w	w	m	w	w	v
c	c	c	o	u	c
a	e	a	a	o	a
g	j	g	j	g	g

Skills: Visual discrimination; Noticing details; Recognizing similarities

ALPHABET SKILLS

Look at the first letter in each row.
Look at the rest of the letters in each row.
Circle the ones that are exactly like the first letter.

d	d	d	b	d	p
z	w	z	z	m	z
e	c	e	e	e	o
y	y	y	j	q	y
f	j	f	t	f	f

Skills: Visual discrimination; Noticing details; Recognizing similarities

ALPHABET SKILLS

Look at the first letter in each row.
Look at the rest of the letters in each row.
Circle the ones that are exactly like the first letter.

h	h d b h h
x	x v x x w
i	j i i i l
v	v v v u w
j	j j i y j

Skills: Visual discrimination; Noticing details; Recognizing similarities

ALPHABET SKILLS

Look at the first letter in each row.
Look at the rest of the letters in each row.
Circle the ones that are exactly like the first letter.

u	n n u u u
k	k k x t k
l	i l l l k
t	t t l t f
m	w m n m m

Skills: Visual discrimination; Noticing details; Recognizing similarities

ALPHABET SKILLS

Look at the first letter in each row.
Look at the rest of the letters in each row.
Circle the ones that are exactly like the first letter.

n	h n m n n
s	z e s s s
o	o e c o o
p	q p p b p
r	r r n r x

Skills: Visual discrimination; Noticing details; Recognizing similarities

ALPHABET SKILLS

Look at the letter on each race car.
Look at the words above each car.
Circle the ones that begin with that letter.

apple
band
ape

boat
ate
big

cold
comb
boy

down
bed
dark

Skills: Visual discrimination; Letter recognition; Noticing similarities; Understanding letter concepts

Look at the letter on each top.
Look at the words beside each top.
Circle the ones that begin with that letter.

eat
egg
bus

elf
face
fish

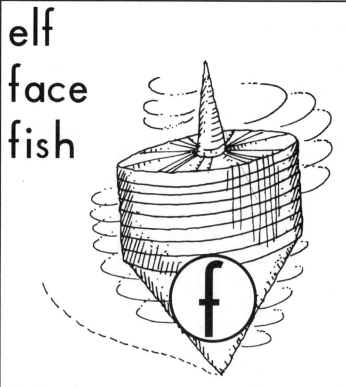

gold
cold
gate

bead
help
hug

Skills: Visual discrimination; Letter recognition; Noticing similarities; Understanding letter concepts

ALPHABET SKILLS

Look at the letter on each baseball cap.
Look at the words beside each cap.
Circle the ones that begin with that letter.

igloo
ice
cat

jump
bump
jet

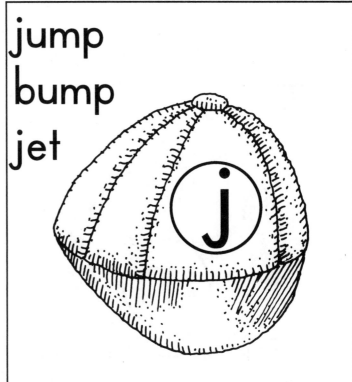

king
kiss
find

face
lace
lip

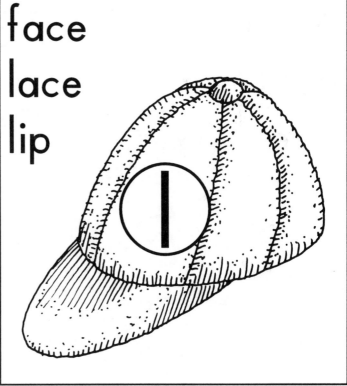

Skills: Visual discrimination; Letter recognition; Noticing similarities; Understanding letter concepts

ALPHABET SKILLS

Look at the letter on each ball.
Look at the words above each ball.
Circle the ones that begin with that letter.

man
map
cap

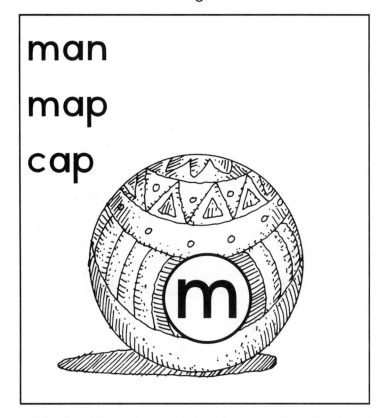

mail
nail
note

open
cold
oven

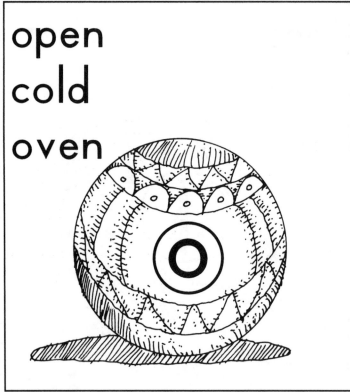

pack
pine
dine

Skills: Visual discrimination; Letter recognition; Noticing similarities; Understanding letter concepts

ALPHABET SKILLS

Look at the letter on each umbrella.
Look at the words beside each umbrella.
Circle the ones that begin with that letter.

quilt
green
quit

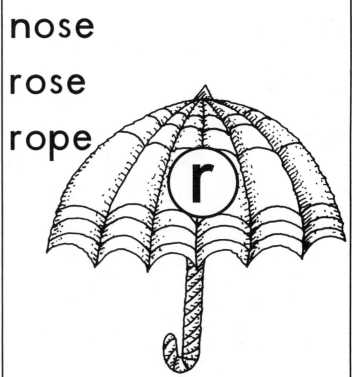

nose
rose
rope

sink
game
same

tail
toad
load

Skills: Visual discrimination; Letter recognition; Noticing similarities; Understanding letter concepts

ALPHABET SKILLS

Look at the letter on each kite.
Look at the words beside each kite.
Circle the ones that begin with that letter.

use
uncle
clue

went
vent
vase

wash
mash
week

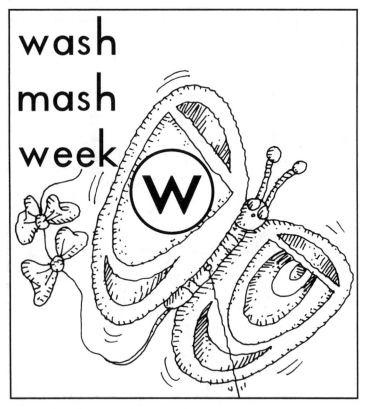

yolk
yam
jam

Skills: Visual discrimination; Letter recognition; Noticing similarities; Understanding letter concepts

ALPHABET SKILLS

Look at the letters in each box.
Find and circle the pairs that are the same letter.

a b
A c

d D
a b

c b
B g

C d
e c

Skills: Visual discrimination; Identifying and matching uppercase and lowercase letters;
Letter recognition

ALPHABET SKILLS

Look at the letters in each box.
Find and circle the pairs that are the same letter.

e E

g f

t e

f F

G g

a q

h d

H f

Skills: Visual discrimination; Identifying and matching uppercase and lowercase letters; Letter recognition

ALPHABET SKILLS

Look at the letters in each box.
Find and circle the pairs that are the same letter.

b	f
I	i

i	J
j	g

k	h
b	K

L	f
l	i

Skills: Visual discrimination; Identifying and matching uppercase and lowercase letters;
Letter recognition

ALPHABET SKILLS

Look at the letters in each box.
Find and circle the pairs that are the same letter.

h m d M	c m N n
a O o c	P j p g

Skills: Visual discrimination; Identifying and matching uppercase and lowercase letters; Letter recognition

ALPHABET SKILLS

Look at the letters in each box.
Find and circle the pairs that are the same letter.

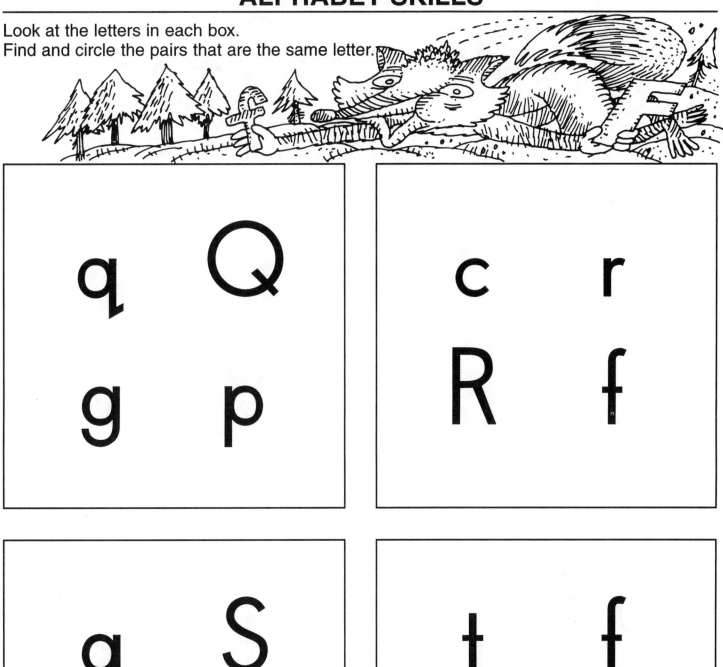

Skills: Visual discrimination; Identifying and matching uppercase and lowercase letters; Letter recognition

ALPHABET SKILLS

Look at the letters in each box.
Find and circle the pairs that are the same letter.

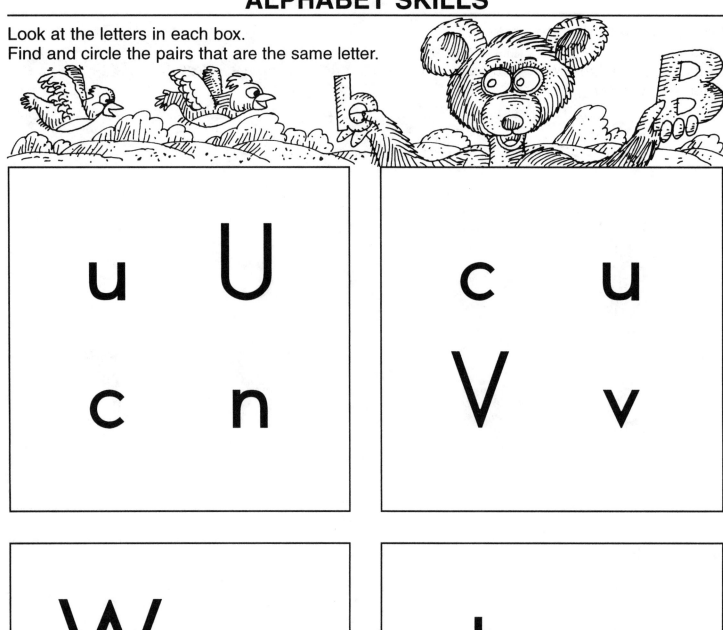

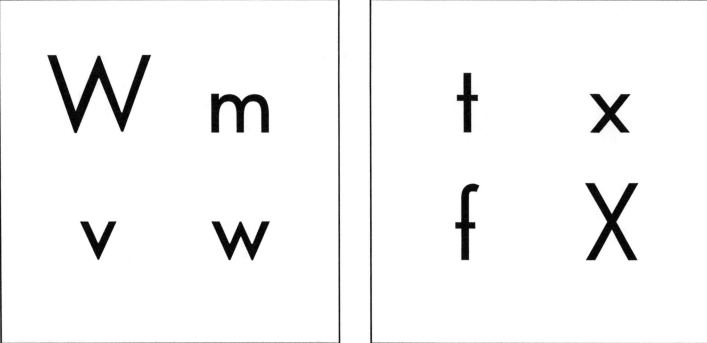

Skills: Visual discrimination; Identifying and matching uppercase and lowercase letters;
Letter recognition

ALPHABET SKILLS

Look at the letters in the top boxes.
Find and circle the letters that are pairs.
In the bottom boxes, write two pairs of uppercase and lowercase letters.
Then ask someone to circle the pairs.

Y   y
j   g

Z   s
n   Z

_____ _____

_____ _____

_____ _____

_____ _____

Skills: Visual discrimination; Identifying and matching uppercase and lowercase letters;
Letter recognition; Creating letter puzzles

ALPHABET SKILLS

Connect the dots from **a** to **z** to find out who is lying in the sun.
Then color the picture.

Skills: Letter order; Recognition of lowercase letters; Fine motor skills

ALPHABET SKILLS

Connect the dots from **A** to **Z** to find out who is juggling all these balls.
Then color the picture.

Skills: Letter order; Recognition of uppercase letters; Fine motor skills

BEGINNING CONSONANTS

Initial consonant: **b**

Bone begins with a **b**.
Look at the other pictures.
Color those whose names begin with a **b**.

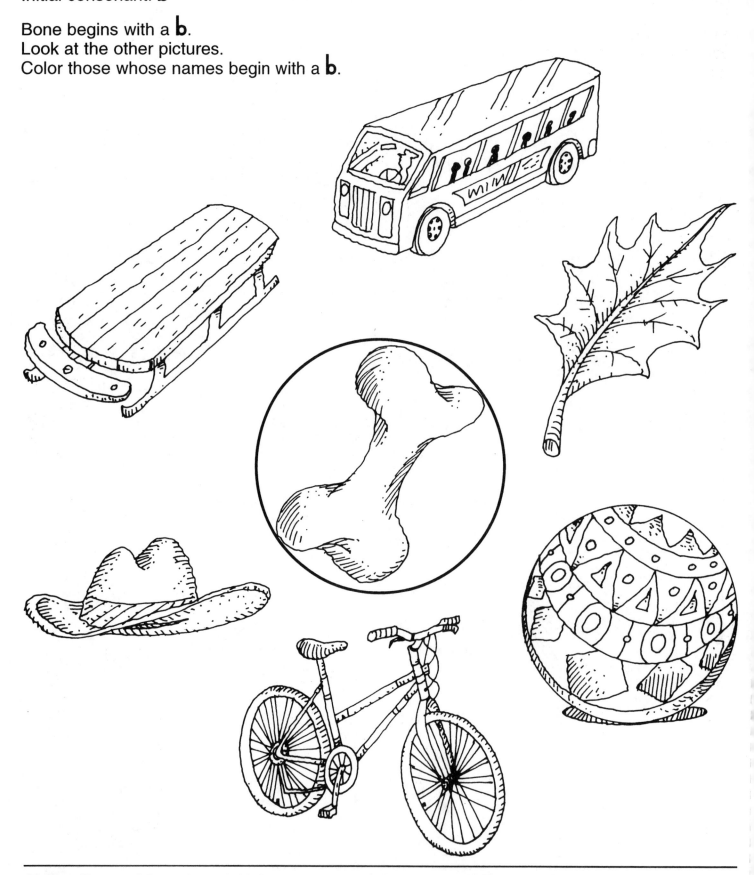

Skills: Recognition of the initial consonant "b"; Sound/symbol association; Auditory discrimination

BEGINNING CONSONANTS

Initial consonant: **c**

Car begins with a **c**.
Look at the other pictures.
Color those whose names begin with a **c**.

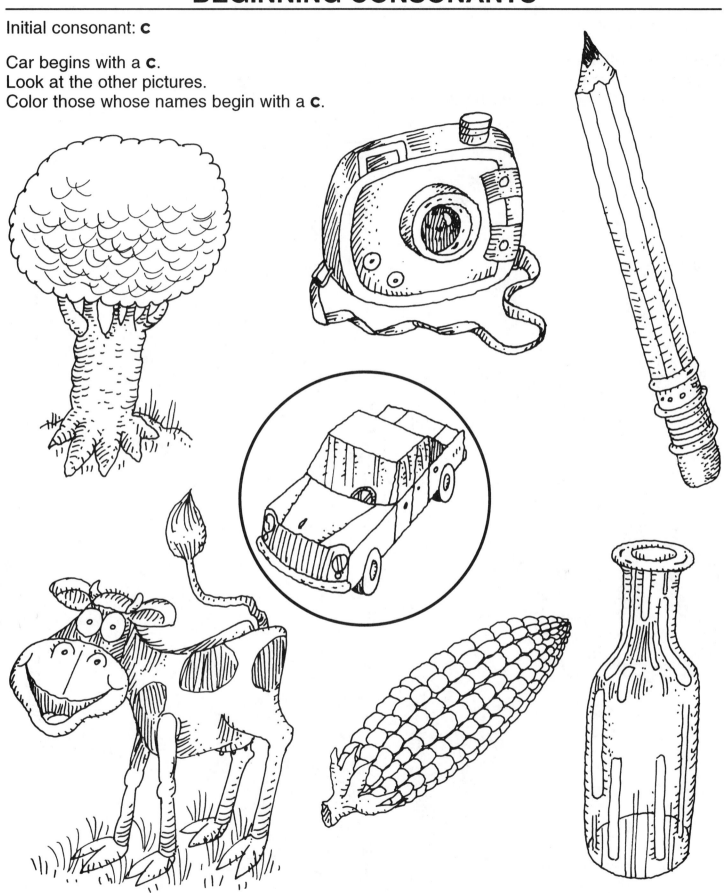

Skills: Recognition of the initial consonant "c"; Sound/symbol association; Auditory discrimination

BEGINNING CONSONANTS

Initial consonant: **d**

Doll begins with a **d**.
Look at the other pictures.
Color those whose names begin with a **d**.

Skills: Recognition of the initial consonant "d"; Sound/symbol association; Auditory discrimination

BEGINNING CONSONANTS

Initial consonant: **f**

Feather begins with an **f**.
Look at the other pictures.
Color those whose names begin with an **f**.

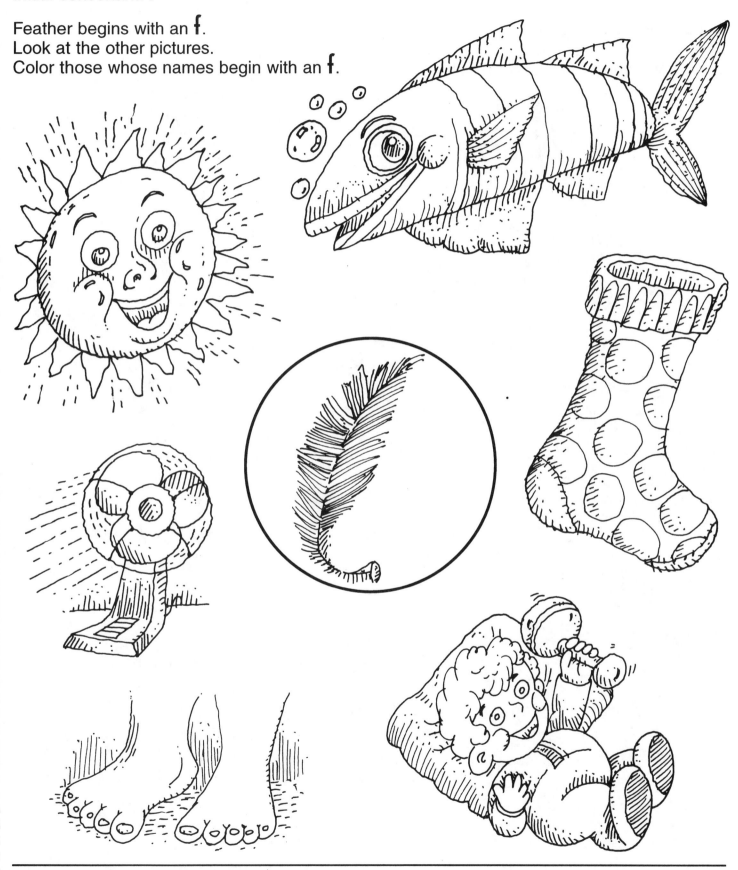

Skills: Recognition of the initial consonant "f"; Sound/symbol association; Auditory discrimination

BEGINNING CONSONANTS

Initial consonant: **g**

Ghost begins with a **g**.
Look at the other pictures.
Color those whose names begin with a **g**.

Skills: Recognition of the initial consonant "g"; Sound/symbol association; Auditory discrimination

BEGINNING CONSONANTS

Initial consonant: h

Horse begins with an h.
Look at the other pictures.
Color those whose names begin with an h.

Skills: Recognition of the initial consonant "h"; Sound/symbol association; Auditory discrimination

BEGINNING CONSONANTS

Initial consonant: **j**

Jack-in-the-box begins with a **j**.
Look at the other pictures.
Color those whose names begin with a **j**.

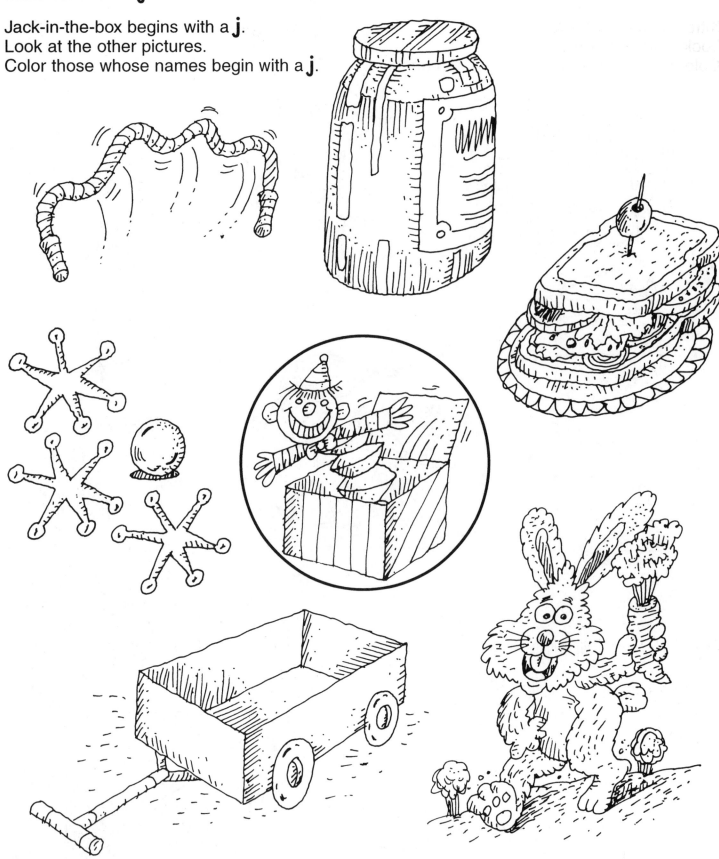

Skills: Recognition of the initial consonant "j"; Sound/symbol association; Auditory discrimination

BEGINNING CONSONANTS

Initial consonant: **k**

Kitten begins with a **k**.
Look at the other pictures.
Color those whose names begin with a **k**.

Skills: Recognition of the initial consonant "k"; Sound/symbol association; Auditory discrimination

BEGINNING CONSONANTS

Initial consonant: l

Ladder begins with an l.
Look at the other pictures.
Color those whose names begin with an l.

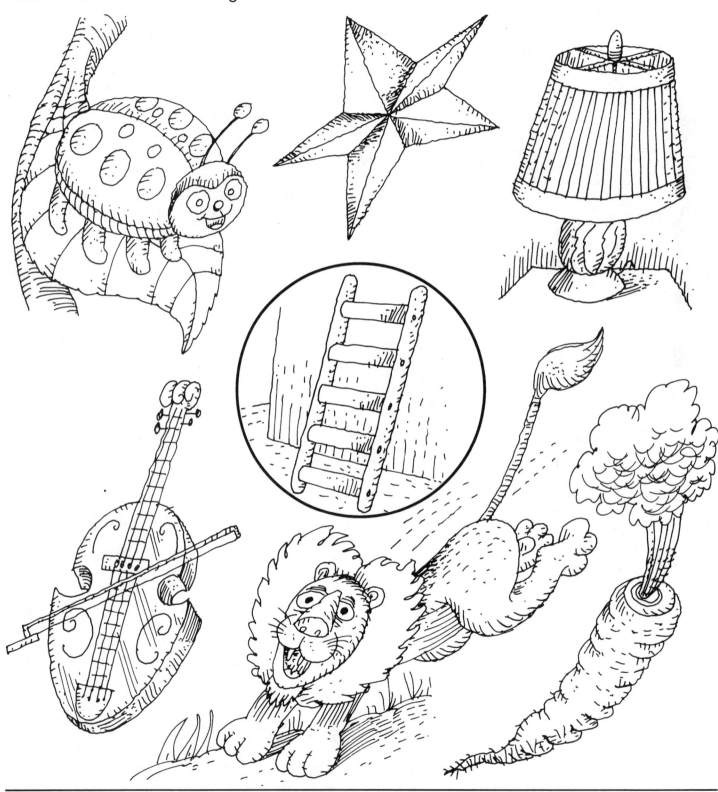

Skills: Recognition of the initial consonant "l"; Sound/symbol association; Auditory discrimination

BEGINNING CONSONANTS

Initial consonant: **m**

Milk begins with an **m**.
Look at the other pictures.
Color those whose names begin with an **m**.

Skills: Recognition of the initial consonant "m"; Sound/symbol association; Auditory discrimination

BEGINNING CONSONANTS

Initial consonant: **n**

Necklace begins with an **n**.
Look at the other pictures.
Color those whose names begin with an **n**.

Skills: Recognition of the initial consonant "n"; Sound/symbol association; Auditory discrimination

BEGINNING CONSONANTS

Initial consonant: **p**

Pie begins with a **p**.
Look at the other pictures.
Color those whose names begin with a **p**.

Skills: Recognition of the initial consonant "p"; Sound/symbol association; Auditory discrimination

BEGINNING CONSONANTS

Initial consonant: **q**

Question mark begins with a **q**.
Look at the other pictures.
Color those whose names begin with a **q**.

Skills: Recognition of the initial consonant "**q**"; Sound/symbol association; Auditory discrimination

BEGINNING CONSONANTS

Initial consonant: **r**

Robot begins with an **r**.
Look at the other pictures.
Color those whose names begin with an **r**.

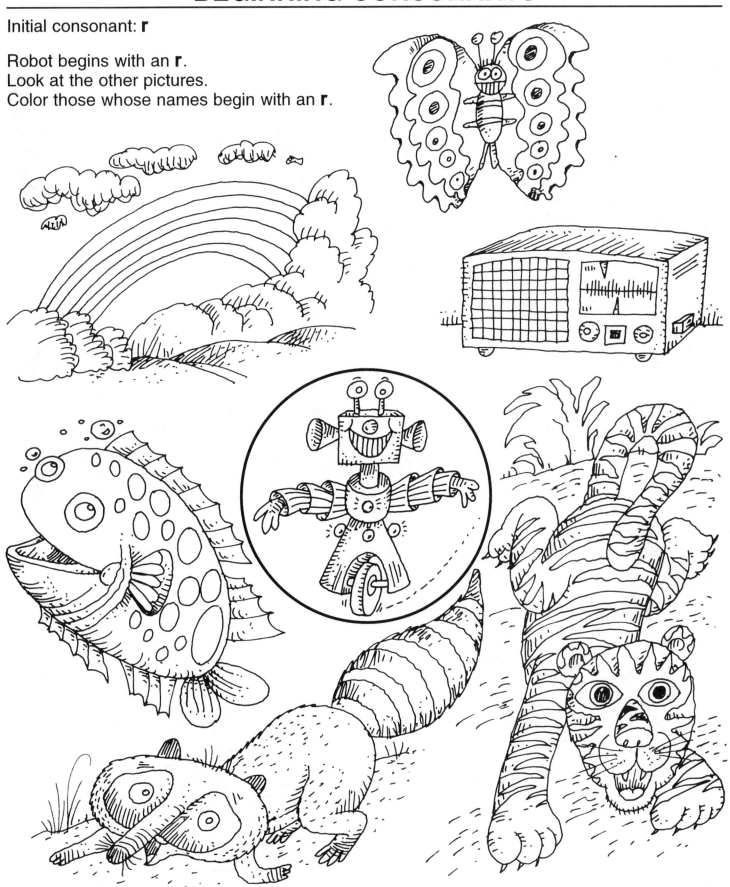

Skills: Recognition of the initial consonant "r"; Sound/symbol association; Auditory discrimination

BEGINNING CONSONANTS

Initial consonant: **s**

Seal begins with an **s**.
Look at the other pictures.
Color those whose names begin with an **s**.

Skills: Recognition of the initial consonant "s"; Sound/symbol association; Auditory discrimination

BEGINNING CONSONANTS

Initial consonant: t

Telephone begins with a t.
Look at the other pictures.
Color those whose names begin with a t.

Skills: Recognition of the initial consonant "t"; Sound/symbol association; Auditory discrimination

BEGINNING CONSONANTS

Initial consonant: **v**

Van begins with a **v**.
Look at the other pictures.
Color those whose names begin with a **v**.

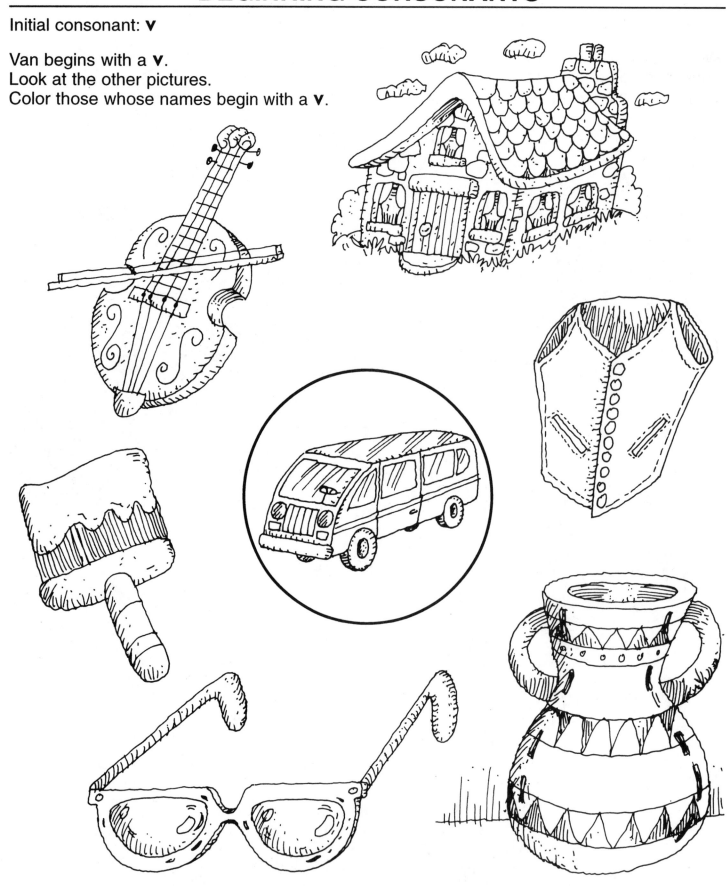

Skills: Recognition of the initial consonant "v"; Sound/symbol association; Auditory discrimination

BEGINNING CONSONANTS

Initial consonant: **w**

Wolf begins with a **w**.
Look at the other pictures.
Color those whose names begin with a **w**.

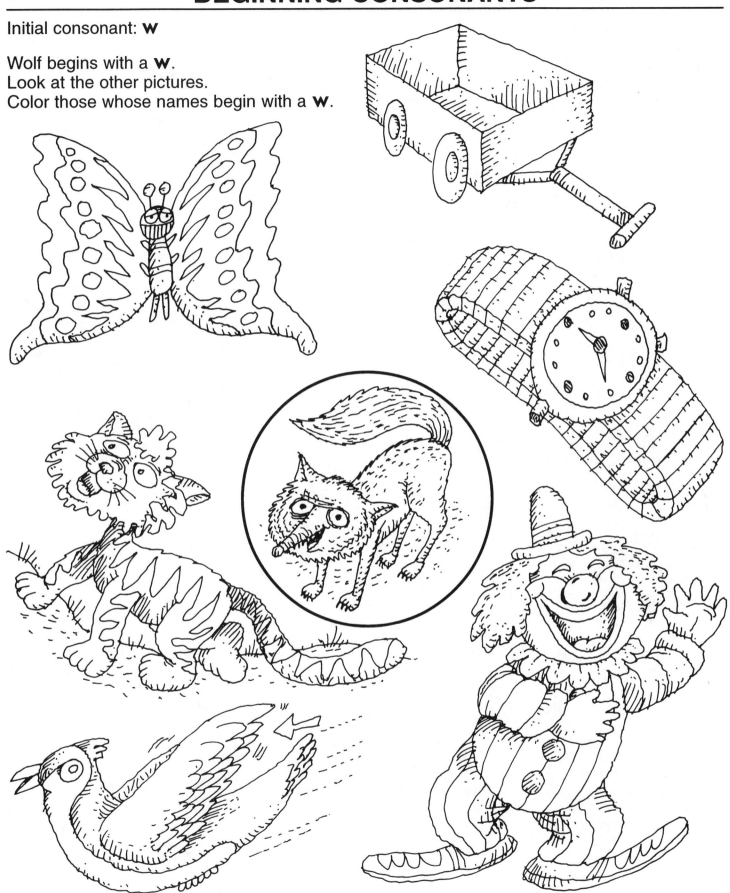

Skills: Recognition of the initial consonant "w"; Sound/symbol association; Auditory discrimination

BEGINNING CONSONANTS

Initial consonant: **y**

Yogurt begins with a **y**.
Look at the other pictures.
Color those whose names begin with a **y**.

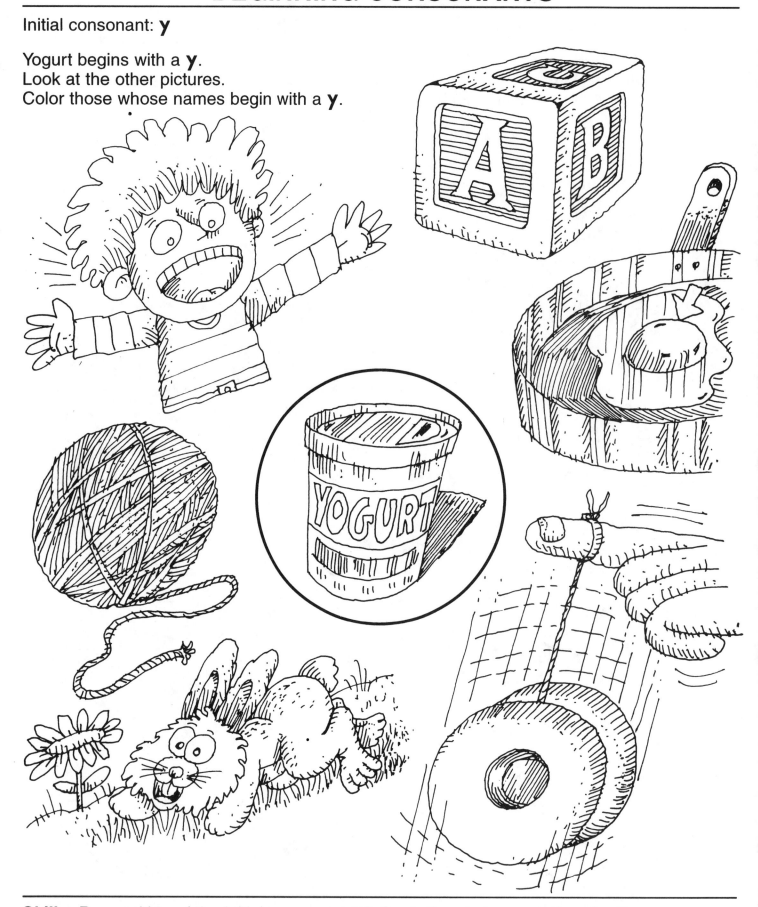

Skills: Recognition of the initial consonant "y"; Sound/symbol association; Auditory discrimination

BEGINNING CONSONANTS

Initial consonant: **z**

Zipper begins with a **z**.
Look at the other pictures.
Color those whose names begin with a **z**.

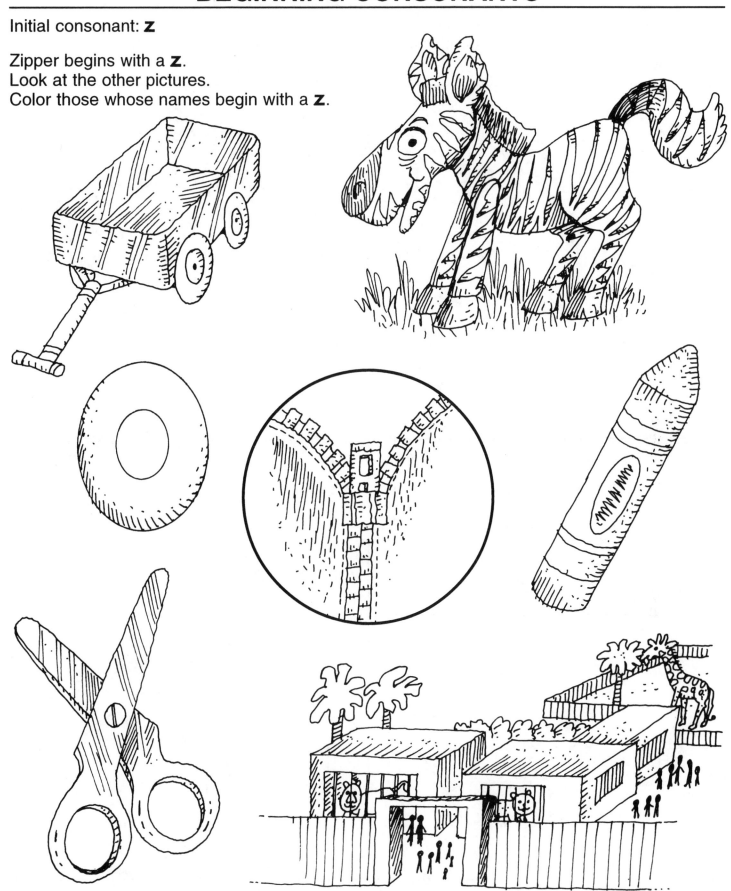

Skills: Recognition of the initial consonant "z"; Sound/symbol association; Auditory discrimination

BEGINNING CONSONANTS

Look at each picture below.
Trace the letter that makes the sound you hear at the beginning of each word.
Then color the pictures.

Skills: Recognition of initial consonants; Sound/symbol association; Writing letters; Auditory discrimination

BEGINNING CONSONANTS

Look at each picture below.
Trace the letter that makes the sound you hear at the beginning of each word.
Then color the pictures.

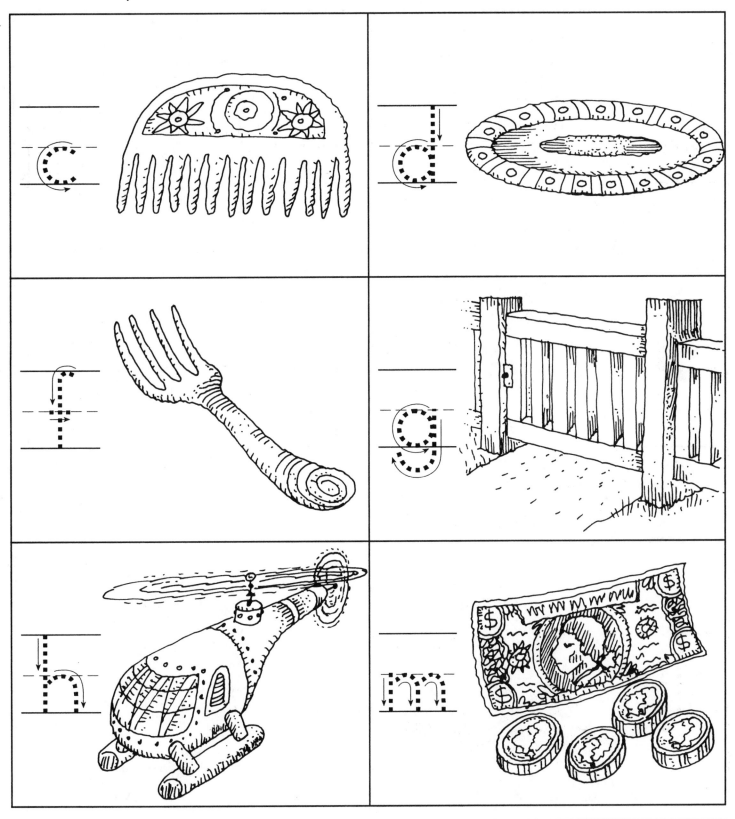

Skills: Recognition of initial consonants; Sound/symbol association; Writing letters; Auditory discrimination

BEGINNING CONSONANTS

Look at each picture below.
Trace the letter that makes the sound you hear at the beginning of each word.
Then color the pictures.

Skills: Recognition of initial consonants; Sound/symbol association; Writing letters; Auditory discrimination

BEGINNING CONSONANTS

Look at each picture below.
Trace the letter that makes the sound you hear at the beginning of each word.
Then color the pictures.

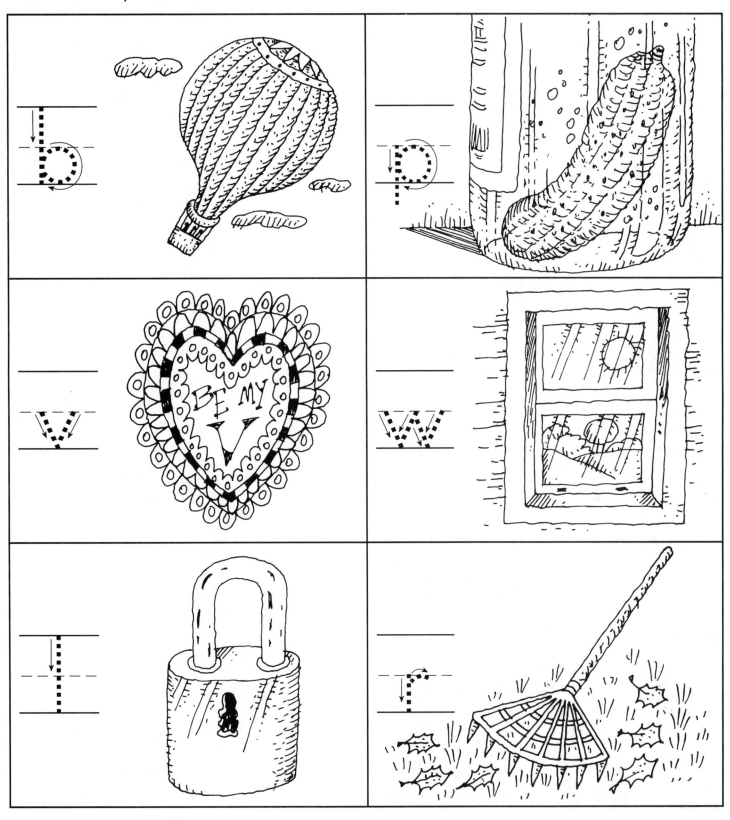

Skills: Recognition of initial consonants; Sound/symbol association; Writing letters; Auditory discrimination

BEGINNING CONSONANTS

Look at the pictures on the left.
Look at the pictures on the right.
Draw lines to match the pictures that begin with the same sound.
Then color the pictures.

Skills: Recognition of initial consonant sounds; Auditory discrimination

BEGINNING CONSONANTS

Look at the pictures on the left.
Look at the pictures on the right.
Draw lines to match the pictures that begin with the same sound.
Then color the pictures.

CHEWING GUM

BEGINNING CONSONANTS

Look at the pictures on the left.
Look at the pictures on the right.
Draw lines to match the pictures that begin with the same sound.
Then color the pictures.

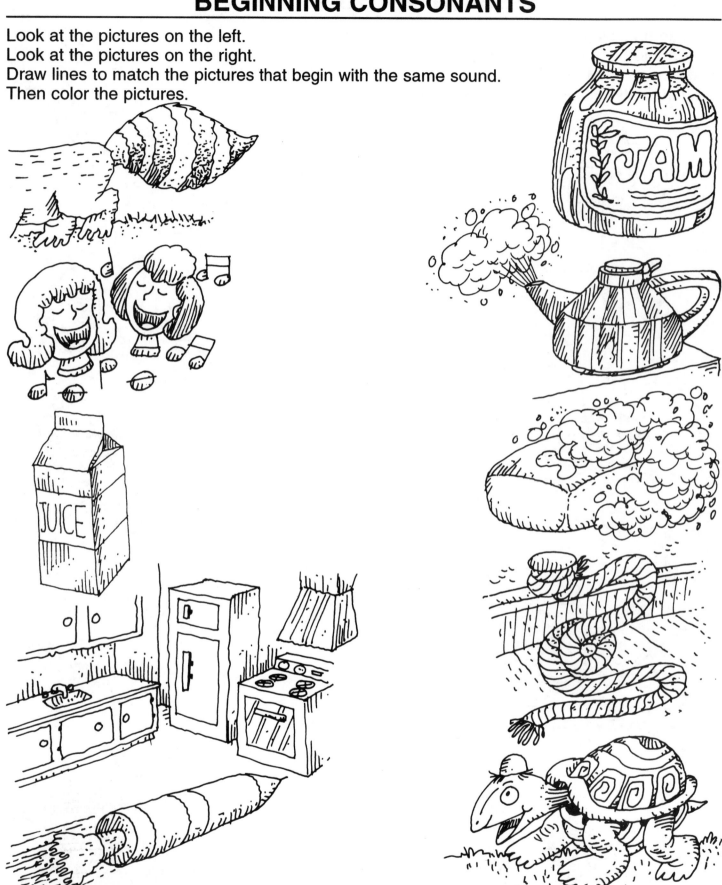

Skills: Recognition of initial consonant sounds; Auditory discrimination

BEGINNING CONSONANTS

Look at the pictures on the left.
Look at the pictures on the right.
Draw lines to match the pictures that begin with the same sound.
Then color the pictures.

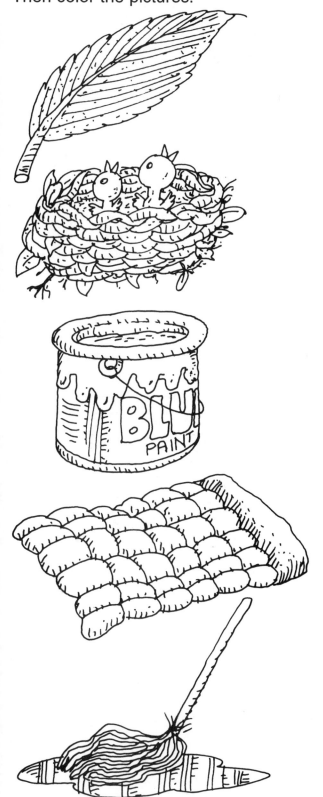

Skills: Recognition of initial consonant sounds; Auditory discrimination

BEGINNING CONSONANTS

Name the picture in each box.
What sound do you hear at the beginning of each word?
Think of a word that has the same beginning sound.
Draw a picture of that word.

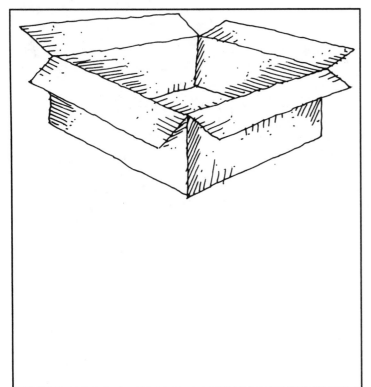

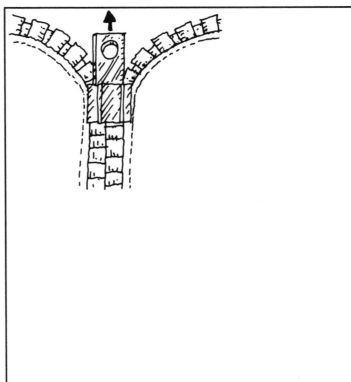

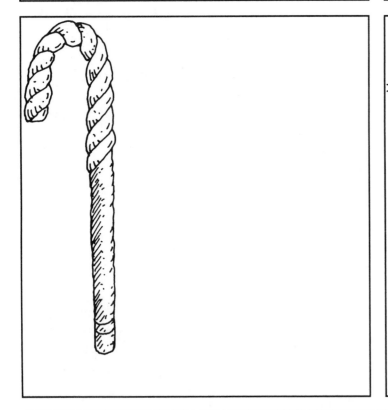

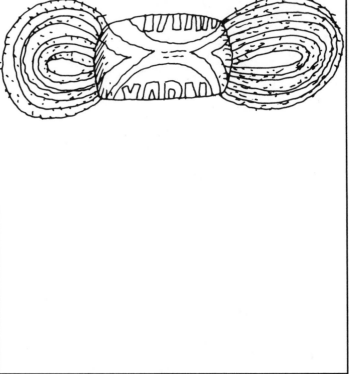

Skills: Recognition of initial consonant sounds; Understanding and extending a concept

BEGINNING CONSONANTS

Name the picture in each box.
What sound do you hear at the beginning of each word?
Think of a word that has the same beginning sound.
Draw a picture of that word.

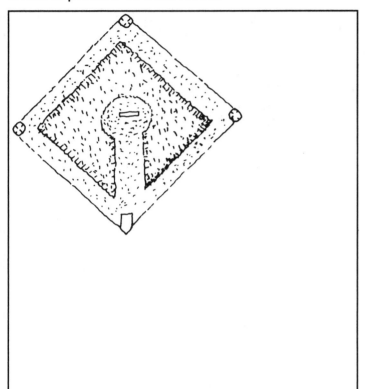

Skills: Recognition of initial consonant sounds; Understanding and extending a concept

BEGINNING CONSONANTS

Name the picture in each box.
What sound do you hear at the beginning of each word?
Think of a word that has the same beginning sound.
Draw a picture of that word.

Skills: Recognition of initial consonant sounds; Understanding and extending a concept

BEGINNING CONSONANTS

Name the picture in each box.
What sound do you hear at the beginning of each word?
Think of a word that has the same beginning sound.
Draw a picture of that word.

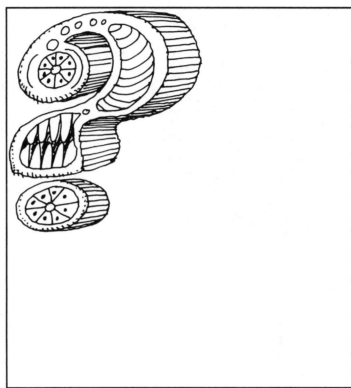

Skills: Recognition of initial consonant sounds; Understanding and extending a concept

BEGINNING CONSONANTS

Name the picture in each box.
What sound do you hear at the beginning of each word?
Think of a word that has the same beginning sound.
Draw a picture of that word.

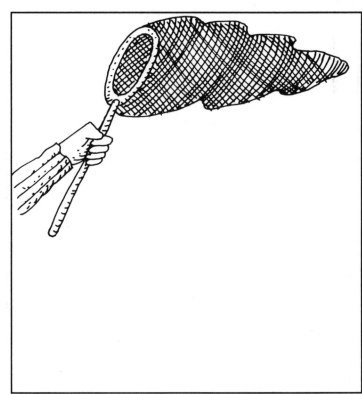

Skills: Recognition of initial consonant sounds; Understanding and extending a concept

BEGINNING CONSONANTS

Name the letter in each box.
What sound does that letter make?
Think of a word that begins with that sound.
Draw a picture of that word.

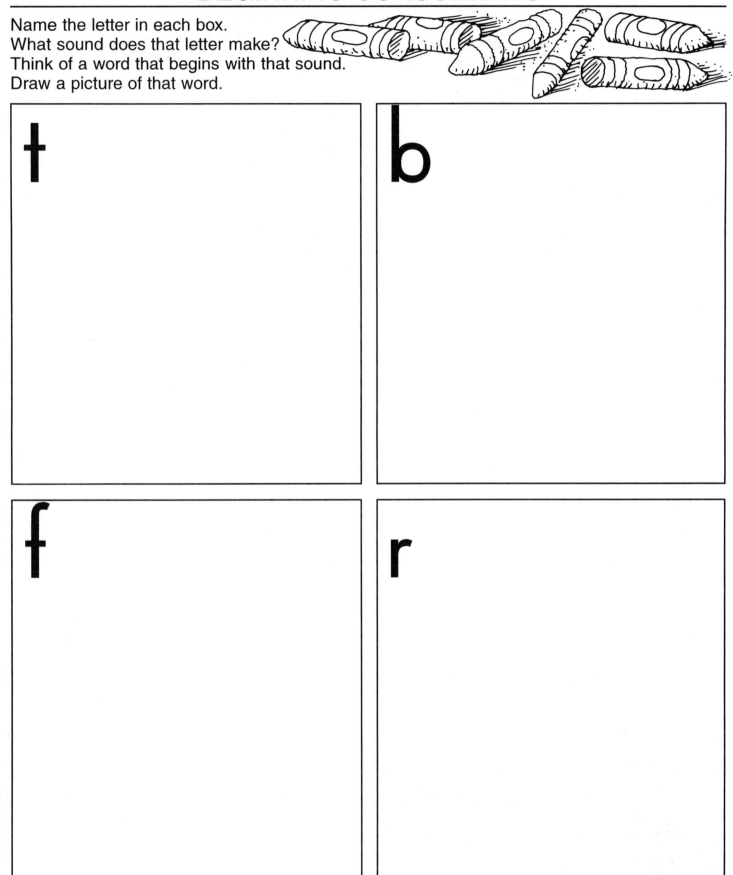

t

b

f

r

Skills: Recognizing letters and their sounds; Understanding and extending a concept

BEGINNING CONSONANTS

Name the letter in each box.
What sound does that letter make?
Think of a word that begins with that sound.
Draw a picture of that word.

C

Z

V

j

Skills: Recognizing letters and their sounds; Understanding and extending a concept

BEGINNING CONSONANTS

Name the letter in each box.
What sound does that letter make?
Think of a word that begins with that sound.
Draw a picture of that word.

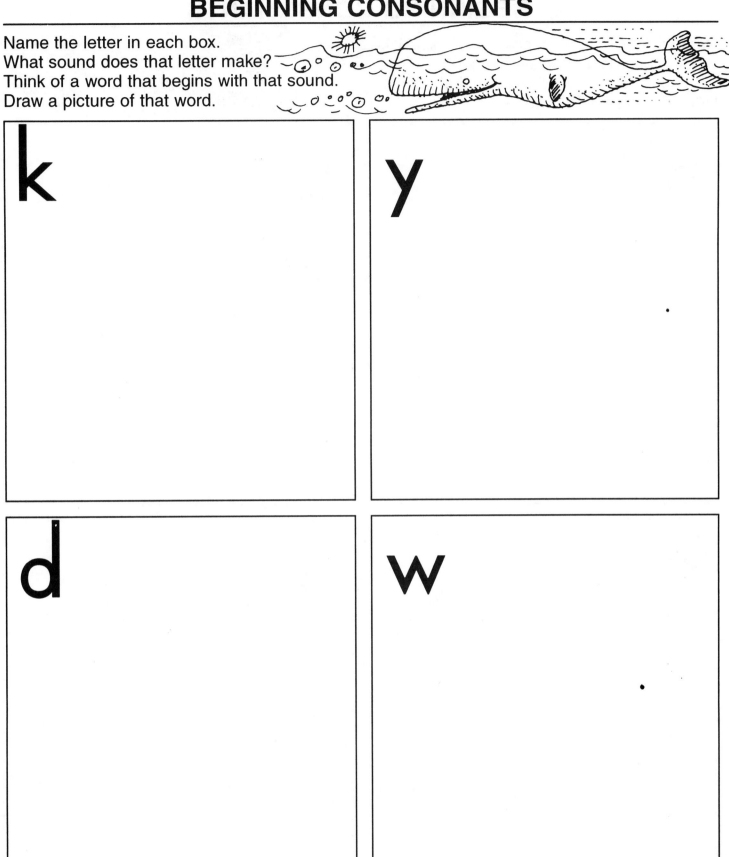

k

y

d

w

Skills: Recognizing letters and their sounds; Understanding and extending a concept

BEGINNING CONSONANTS

Name the letter in each box.
What sound does that letter make?
Think of a word that begins with that sound.
Draw a picture of that word.

n	g
q	h

Skills: Recognizing letters bend their sounds; Understanding and extending a concept

BEGINNING CONSONANTS

Name the letter in each box.
What sound does that letter make?
Think of a word that begins with that sound.
Draw a picture of that word.

l

m

s

p

Skills: Recognizing letters bend their sounds; Understanding and extending a concept

BEGINNING CONSONANTS

Look at the letters at the top of the page.
Then look at the pictures on this page.
Write the letter that makes the sound you hear at the beginning of each word.
Then color the pictures.

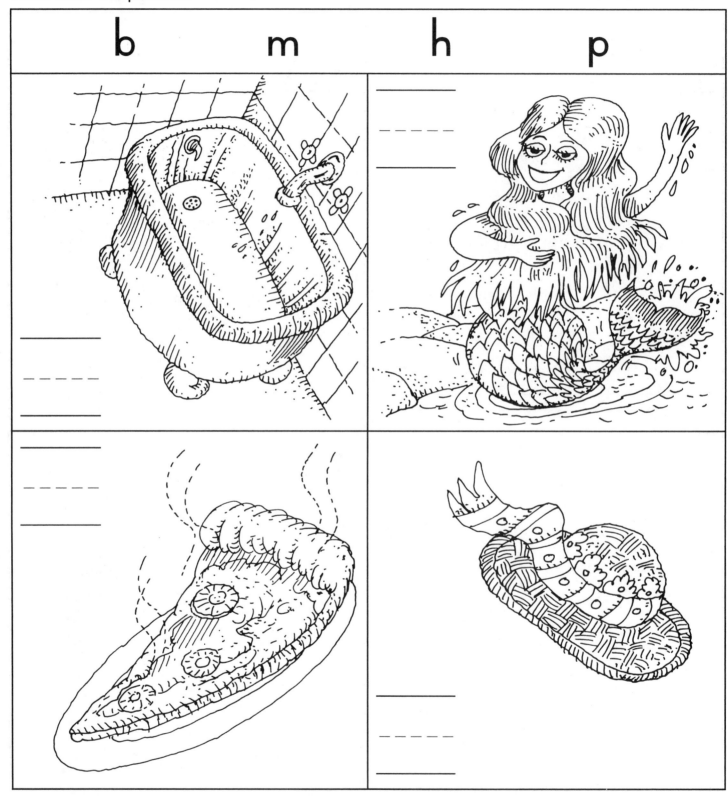

b   m   h   p

Skills: Recognizing letters and their sounds; Sound/symbol association; Writing letters

BEGINNING CONSONANTS

Look at the letters at the top of the page.
Then look at the pictures on this page.
Write the letter that makes the sound you hear at the beginning of each word.
Then color the pictures.

r   s   f   g

Skills: Recognizing letters and their sounds; Sound/symbol association; Writing letters

BEGINNING CONSONANTS

Look at the letters at the top of the page.
Then look at the pictures on this page.
Write the letter that makes the sound you hear at the beginning of each word.
Then color the pictures.

j   k   l   n

Skills: Recognizing letters and their sounds; Sound/symbol association; Writing letters

BEGINNING CONSONANTS

Look at the letters at the top of the page.
Then look at the pictures on this page.
Write the letter that makes the sound you hear at the beginning of each word.
Then color the pictures.

c   d   q   t

Skills: Recognizing letters bend their sounds; Sound/symbol association; Writing letters

BEGINNING CONSONANTS

Look at the letters at the top of the page.
Then look at the pictures on this page.
Write the letter that makes the sound you hear at the beginning of each word.
Then color the pictures.

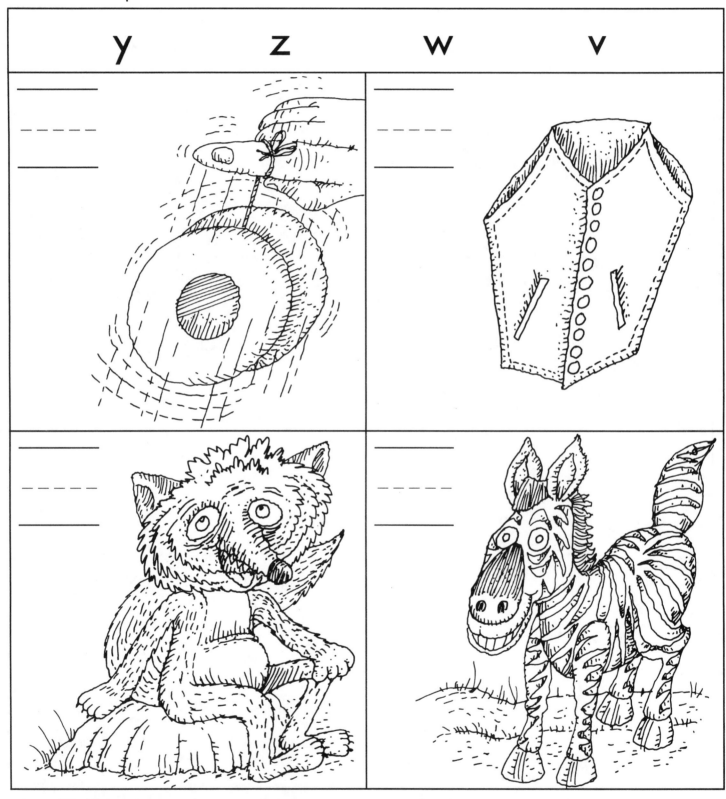

Skills: Recognizing letters and their sounds; Sound/symbol association; Writing letters

BEGINNING CONSONANTS

Look at the letter in each small box.
Then look at the pictures in each large box.
Color the pictures that begin with the letter in each small box.

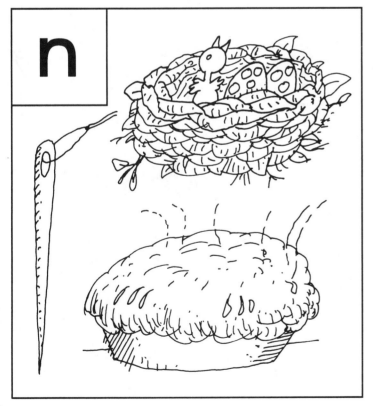

Skills: Recognizing letters and their sounds; Sound/symbol association; Identifying initial consonants

BEGINNING CONSONANTS

Look at the letter in each small box.
Then look at the pictures in each large box.
Color the pictures that begin with the letter in each small box.

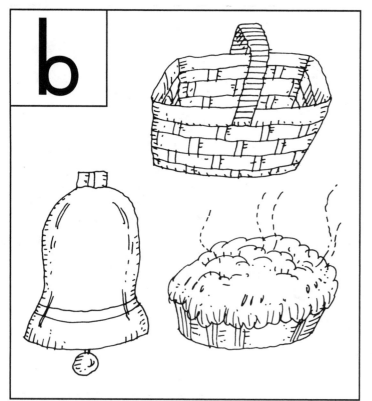

Skills: Recognizing letters and their sounds; Sound/symbol association; Identifying initial consonants

BEGINNING CONSONANTS

Look at the letter in each small box.
Then look at the pictures in each large box.
Color the pictures that begin with the letter in each small box.

r
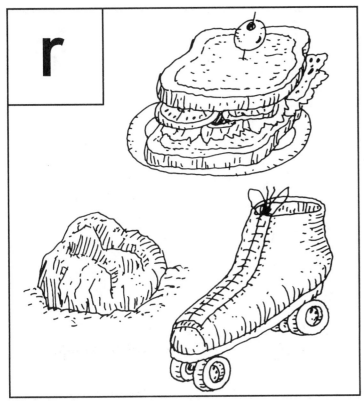

f
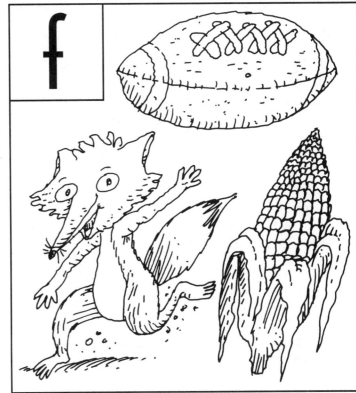

k
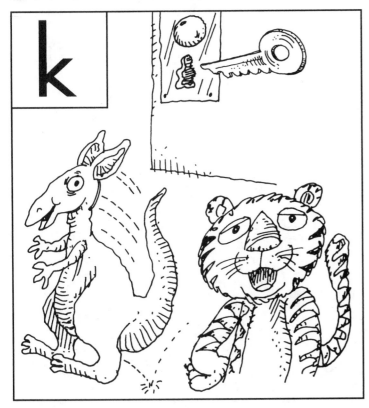

y
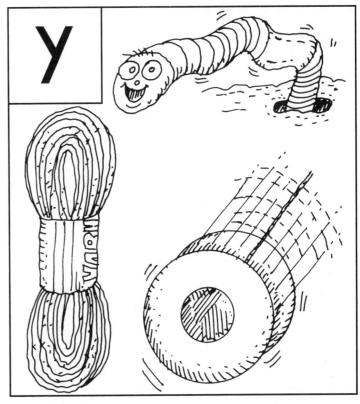

Skills: Recognizing letters and their sounds; Sound/symbol association; Identifying initial consonants

BEGINNING CONSONANTS

Look at the letter in each small box.
Then look at the pictures in each large box.
Color the pictures that begin with the letter in each small box.

h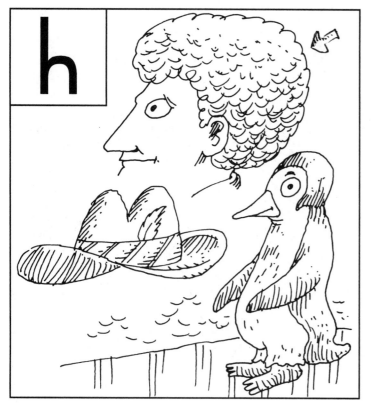

l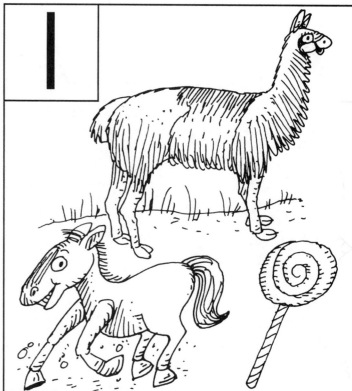

j

z

Skills: Recognizing letters bend their sounds; Sound/symbol association; Identifying initial consonants

BEGINNING CONSONANTS

Look at the letter in each small box.
Then look at the pictures in each large box.
Color the pictures that begin with the letter in each small box.

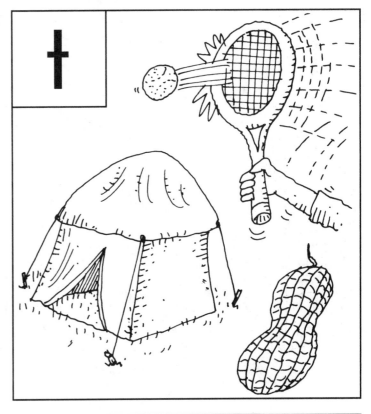

Skills: Recognizing letters and their sounds; Sound/symbol association; Identifying initial consonants

BEGINNING CONSONANTS

Look at the clown's balloons.
Say the name of the picture on each balloon.
Color the balloon blue if the picture begins with a **b**.
Color the balloon purple if the picture begins with a **p**.
Color the balloon red if the picture begins with an **r**.
Color the balloon yellow if the picture begins with a **y**.

Skills: Recognizing letters and their sounds; Sound/symbol association; Identifying initial consonants

BEGINNING CONSONANTS

Look at the beautiful necklace.
Say the name of the picture on each bead.
Color the bead green if the picture begins with a **d**.
Color the bead yellow if the picture begins with an **f**.
Color the bead orange if the picture begins with a **c**.
Color the bead brown if the picture begins with a **g**.

Skills: Recognizing letters bend their sounds; Sound/symbol association; Identifying initial consonants

95

BEGINNING CONSONANTS

What delicious apples!
Say the name of the picture on each apple.
Color the apple red if the picture begins with an **h**.
Color the apple yellow if the picture begins with a **k**.
Color the apple green if the picture begins with a **j**.

BEGINNING CONSONANTS

Look what is in the refrigerator!
Say the names of the pictures on each shelf.
Color the picture red if it begins with a **t**.
Color the picture yellow if it begins with an **l**.
Color the picture white if it begins with an **m**.
Color the picture green if it begins with a **p**.

Skills: Recognizing letters and their sounds; Sound/symbol association; Identifying initial consonants

BEGINNING CONSONANTS

Let's blow some bubbles!
Say the name of the picture inside each bubble.
Color the bubble blue if the picture begins with an **n**.
Color the bubble purple if the picture begins with an **s**.
Color the bubble green if the picture begins with a **w**.

Skills: Recognizing letters and their sounds; Sound/symbol association; Identifying initial consonants

MORE ABOUT CONSONANTS

Final consonants: **d** and **g**

The ending sound in cloud is a **d**. The ending sound in dog is a **g**.
Look at the picture at the beginning of each row.
Color the pictures in that row that end with the same sound.

Skills: Recognition of the final consonants "d" and "g"; Sound/symbol association; Auditory discrimination

MORE ABOUT CONSONANTS

Final consonants: **b** and **t**

The ending sound in web is a **b**. The ending sound in goat is a **t**.
Look at the picture at the beginning of each row.
Color the pictures in that row that end with the same sound.

Skills: Recognition of the final consonants "b" and "t"; Sound/symbol association; Auditory discrimination

MORE ABOUT CONSONANTS

Final consonants: **f** and **k**

The ending sound in chef is an **f**. The ending sound in oak is a **k**.
Look at the picture at the beginning of each row.
Color the pictures in that row that end with the same sound.

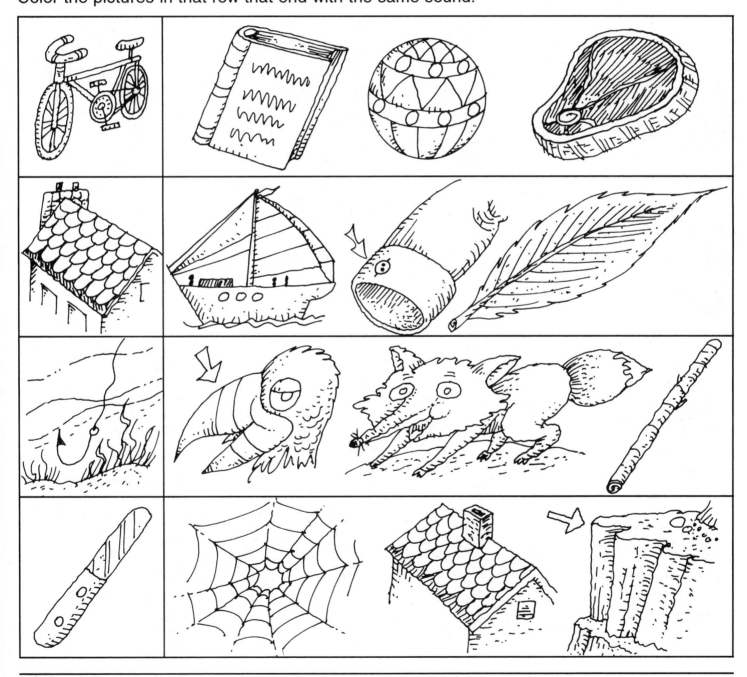

Skills: Recognition of the final consonants "f" and "k"; Sound/symbol association; Auditory discrimination

MORE ABOUT CONSONANTS

Final consonants: **l** and **m**

The ending sound in nail is an **l**. The ending sound in broom is an **m**.
Look at the picture at the beginning of each row.
Color the pictures in that row that end with the same sound.

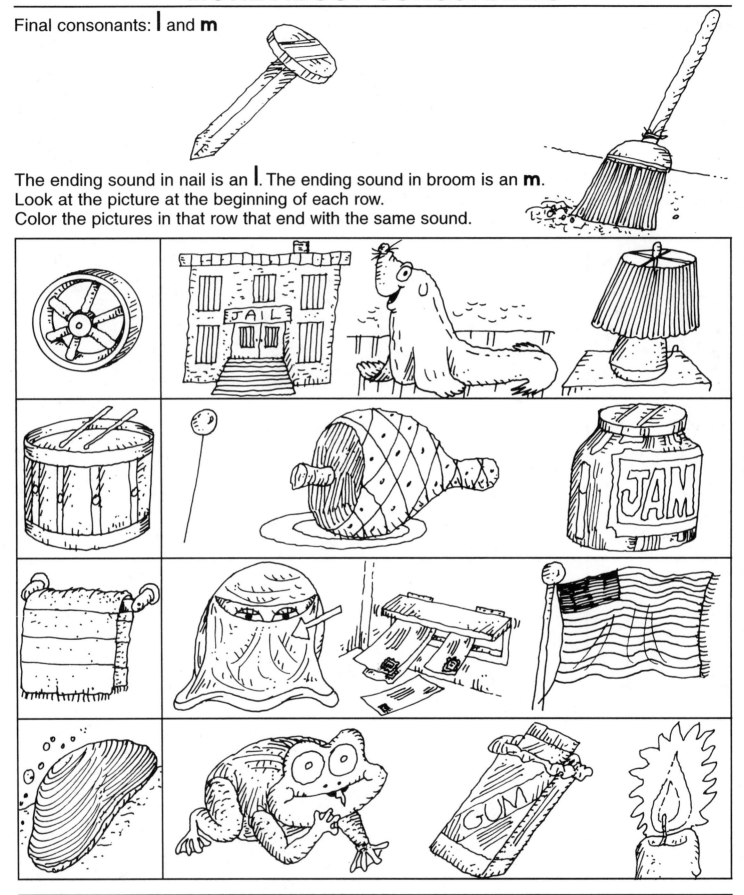

Skills: Recognition of the final consonants "l" and "m"; Sound/symbol association; Auditory discrimination

MORE ABOUT CONSONANTS

Final consonants: **n** and **p**

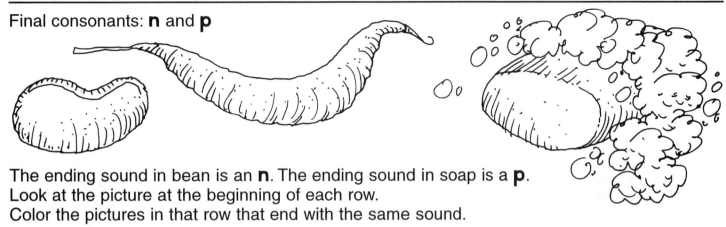

The ending sound in bean is an **n**. The ending sound in soap is a **p**.
Look at the picture at the beginning of each row.
Color the pictures in that row that end with the same sound.

Skills: Recognition of the final consonants "n" and "p"; Sound/symbol association; Auditory discrimination

MORE ABOUT CONSONANTS

Final consonants: **ll** and **ss**

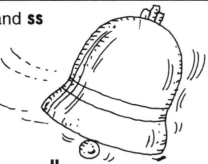

The ending sound in bell is **ll**. The ending sound in dress is **ss**.
Look at the picture at the beginning of each row.
Color the pictures in that row that end with the same sound.

Skills: Recognition of the final consonants "ll" and "ss"; Sound/symbol association; Auditory discrimination

MORE ABOUT CONSONANTS

The hen wants to find her way to the pen.
Follow the path of pictures whose names end with the **n** sound.

Skills: Recognition of the final consonant "n"; Auditory discrimination; Visual perception

MORE ABOUT CONSONANTS

The cat wants to buy a hat.
Color the hats that have pictures whose names end with the **t** sound.

Skills: Recognition of the final consonant "t"; Auditory discrimination; Visual perception

MORE ABOUT CONSONANTS

Look at the letters on the left.
Look at the pictures on the right.
Draw a line to match each letter to the picture that ends with the sound it makes.
Then color the pictures.

x

m

p

s

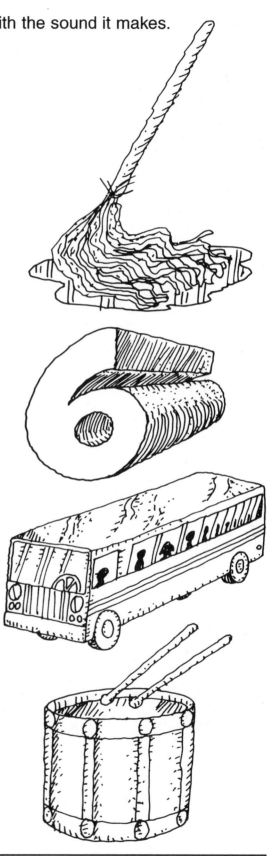

Skills: Recognition of final consonants; Sound/symbol association; Auditory discrimination

MORE ABOUT CONSONANTS

Look at the letters on the left.
Look at the pictures on the right.
Draw a line to match each letter to the picture that ends with the sound it makes.
Then color the pictures.

b

k

n

l

Skills: Recognition of final consonants; Sound/symbol association; Auditory discrimination

MORE ABOUT CONSONANTS

Look at the letters on the left.
Look at the pictures on the right.
Draw a line to match each letter to the picture that ends with the sound it makes.
Then color the pictures.

v

z

f

g

Skills: Recognition of final consonants; Sound/symbol association; Auditory discrimination

MORE ABOUT CONSONANTS

Look at the letters at the top of the page.
Look at the pictures and words.
Write the letter that completes each word.
Then color the pictures.

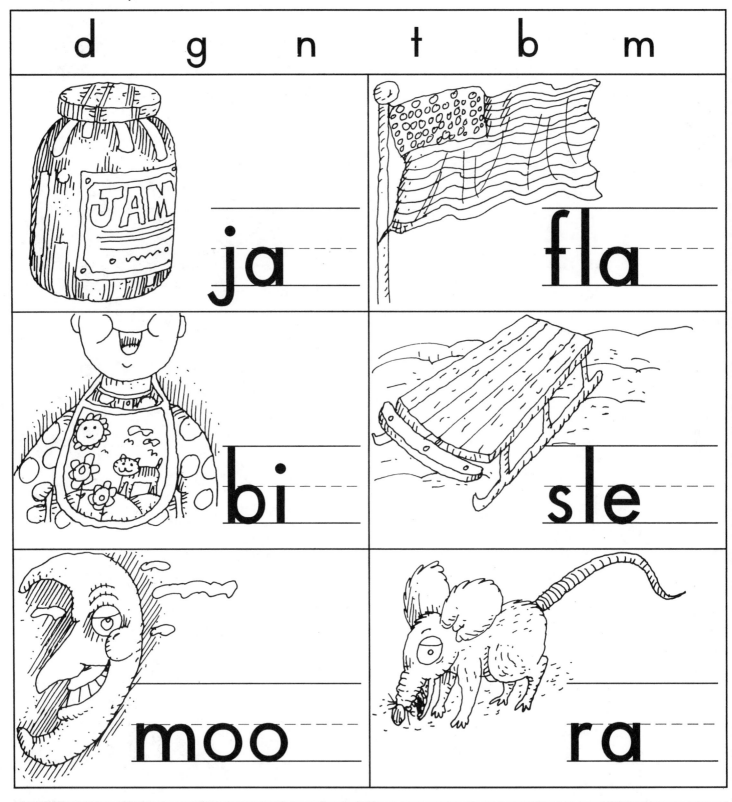

d   g   n   t   b   m

ja____

fla____

bi____

sle____

moo____

ra____

Skills: Recognition of final consonants; Writing letters and words; Association between sounds, symbols, and words

MORE ABOUT CONSONANTS

Look at the letters at the top of the page.
Look at the pictures and words.
Write the letter that completes each word.
Then color the pictures.

f   k   l   p   s   x

bu

boo

bo

lea

soa

pai

Skills: Recognition of final consonants; Writing letters and words; Association between sounds, symbols, and words

MORE ABOUT CONSONANTS

Name the picture in each box.
Look at the letters next to it.
Circle the letter you hear at the end of each word.
Then color the pictures.

Skills: Recognition of final consonants; Auditory discrimination; Association between sounds and symbols

MORE ABOUT CONSONANTS

Name the picture in each box.
Look at the letters next to it.
Circle the letter you hear at the end of each word.
Then color the pictures.

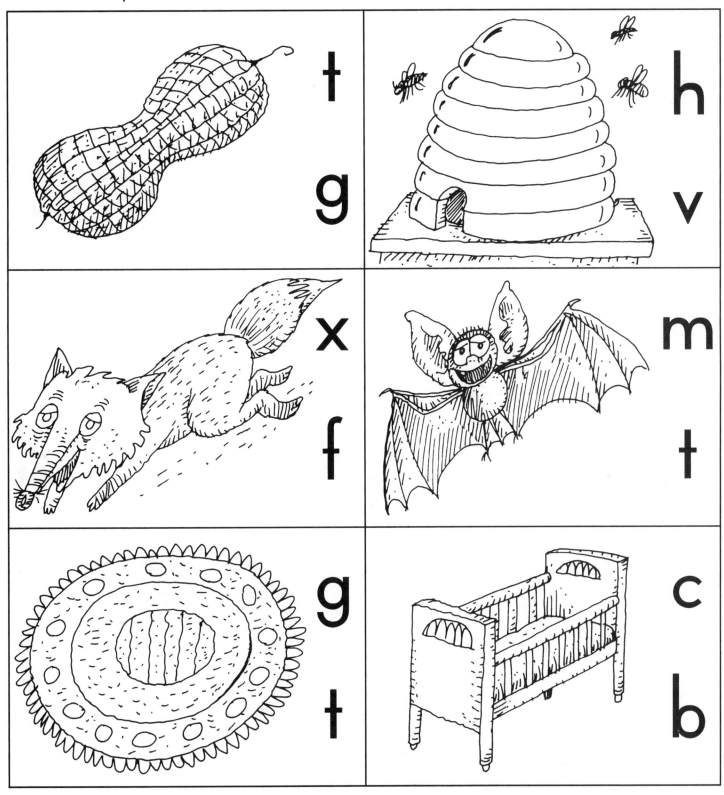

Skills: Recognition of final consonants; Auditory discrimination; Association between sounds and symbols

113

MORE ABOUT CONSONANTS

Name the picture in each box.
Look at the letters next to it.
Circle the letter you hear at the end of each word.
Then color the pictures.

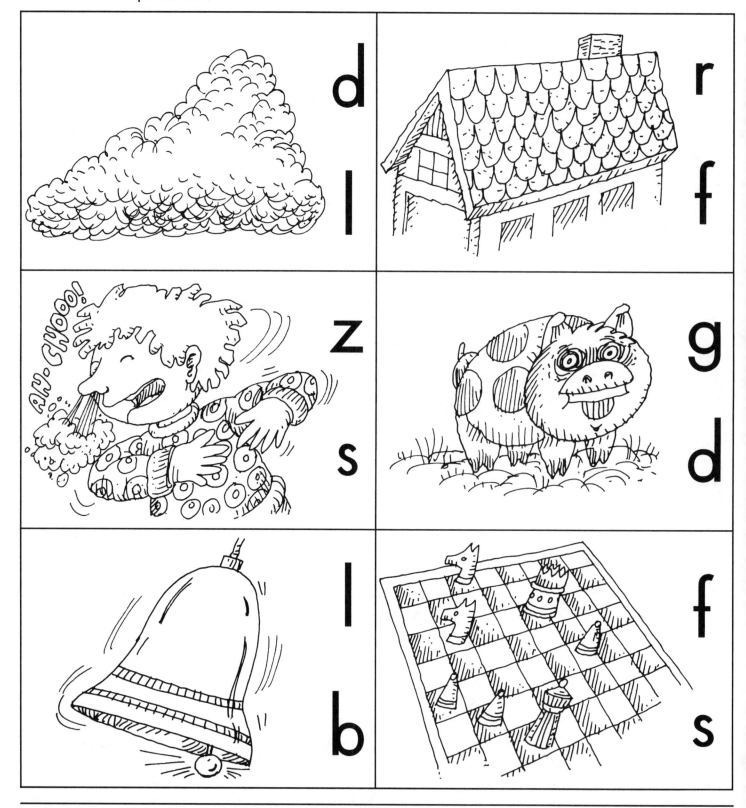

Skills: Recognition of final consonants; Auditory discrimination; Association between sounds and symbols

MORE ABOUT CONSONANTS

Look at the school of fish!
Say the name of the picture inside each fish.
Color the fish red if the picture ends with an **n**.
Color the fish yellow if the picture ends with a **d**.
Color the fish green if the picture ends with a **p**.

Skills: Recognition of letters and their sounds; Sound/symbol association; Identification of final consonants

MORE ABOUT CONSONANTS

Name the picture in each box.
Look at the letters under it.
Circle the letter you hear at the **beginning** of each word.
Draw a line under the letter you hear at the **end** of each word.
Then color the pictures.

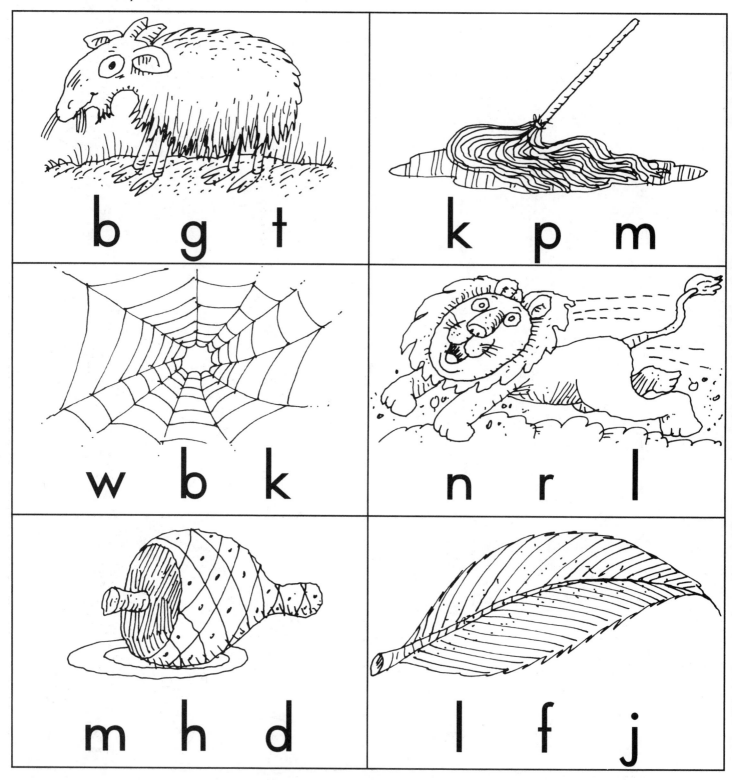

b g t	k p m
w b k	n r l
m h d	l f j

Skills: Recognition of beginning and final consonants; Auditory discrimination; Association between sounds and symbols; Following multiple directions

MORE ABOUT CONSONANTS

Name the picture in each box.
Look at the letters under it.
Circle the letter you hear at the **beginning** of each word.
Draw a line under the letter you hear at the **end** of each word.
Then color the pictures.

b g r

d f n

w d k

x s b

d v n

l v z

Skills: Recognition of beginning and final consonants; Auditory discrimination; Association between sounds and symbols; Following multiple directions

MORE ABOUT CONSONANTS

Look at the picture in each box and say its name.
Name the beginning and ending sounds you hear for each word.
Then write the letters to complete each word.

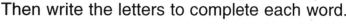

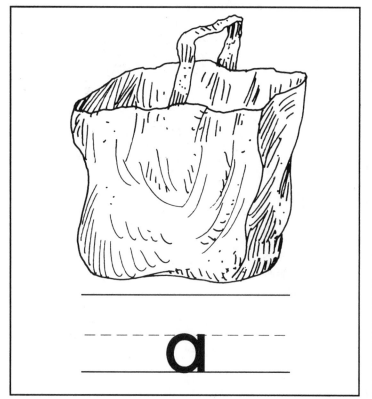

a

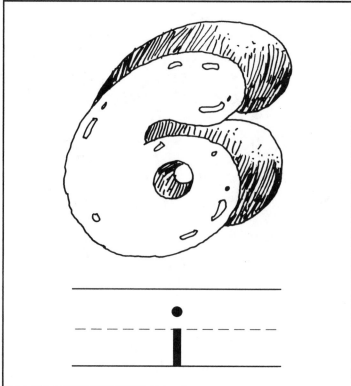

i

u

u

Skills: Recognition of beginning and final consonants; Auditory discrimination; Association between sounds and symbols; Fine motor skills

MORE ABOUT CONSONANTS

Look at the picture in each box and say its name.
Name the beginning and ending sounds you hear for each word.
Then write the letters to complete each word.

___ **a** ___

___ **a** ___

___ **u** ___

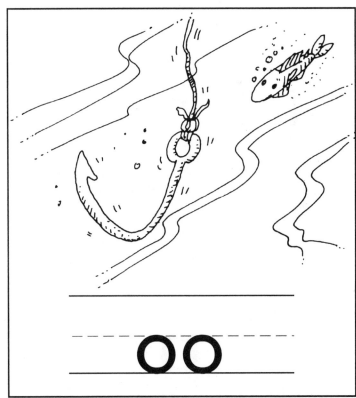

___ **o o** ___

Skills: Recognition of beginning and final consonants; Auditory discrimination; Association between sounds and symbols; Fine motor skills

MORE ABOUT CONSONANTS

Look at the picture in each box and say its name.
Name the beginning and ending sounds you hear for each word.
Then write the letters to complete each word.

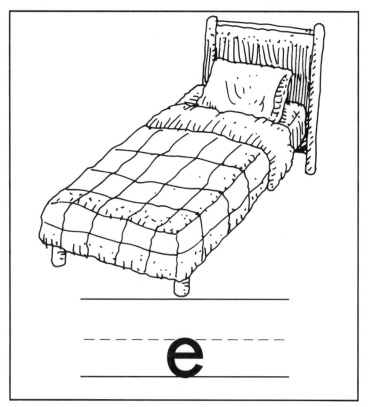

e

ea

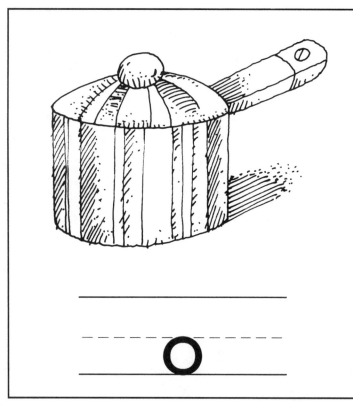

o

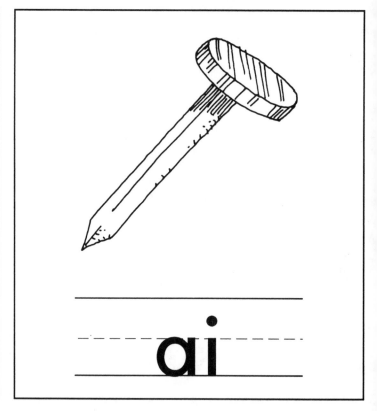

ai

Skills: Recognition of beginning and final consonants; Auditory discrimination; Association between sounds and symbols; Fine motor skills

MORE ABOUT CONSONANTS

Look at all the mittens!
You hear an **m** at the beginning of mitten.
You hear a **t** in the middle of mitten.
You hear an **n** at the end of mitten.
Say the name of the picture on each mitten.
Circle the letter you hear in the middle of each word.

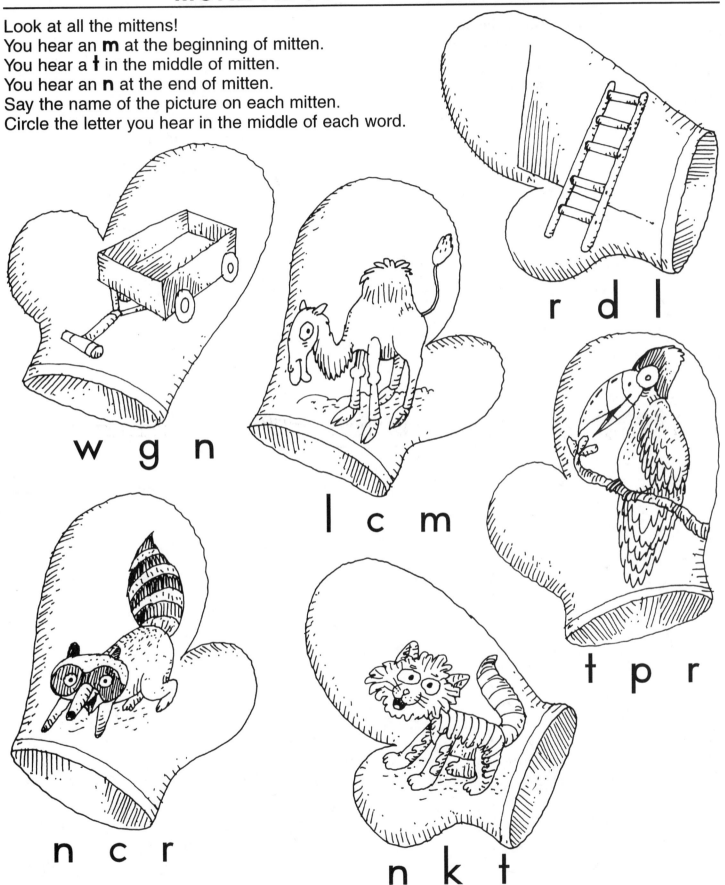

w g n

r d l

l c m

t p r

n c r

n k t

Skills: Auditory discrimination; Recognition of medial consonants; Sound/symbol association

MORE ABOUT CONSONANTS

There are so many pretty tulips!
You hear a **t** at the beginning of tulip.
You hear an **l** in the middle of tulip.
You hear a **p** at the end of tulip.
Say the name of the picture on each tulip.
Circle the letter you hear in the middle of each word.

r t c

l b n

t n p

t d n

t g r

t n l

Skills: Auditory discrimination; Recognition of medial consonants; Sound/symbol association

MORE ABOUT CONSONANTS

Tennis is a fun sport!
You hear a **t** at the beginning of tennis.
You hear an **n** in the middle of tennis.
You hear an **s** at the end of tennis.
Say the name of the picture on each tennis racket or ball.
Circle the letter you hear in the middle of each word.

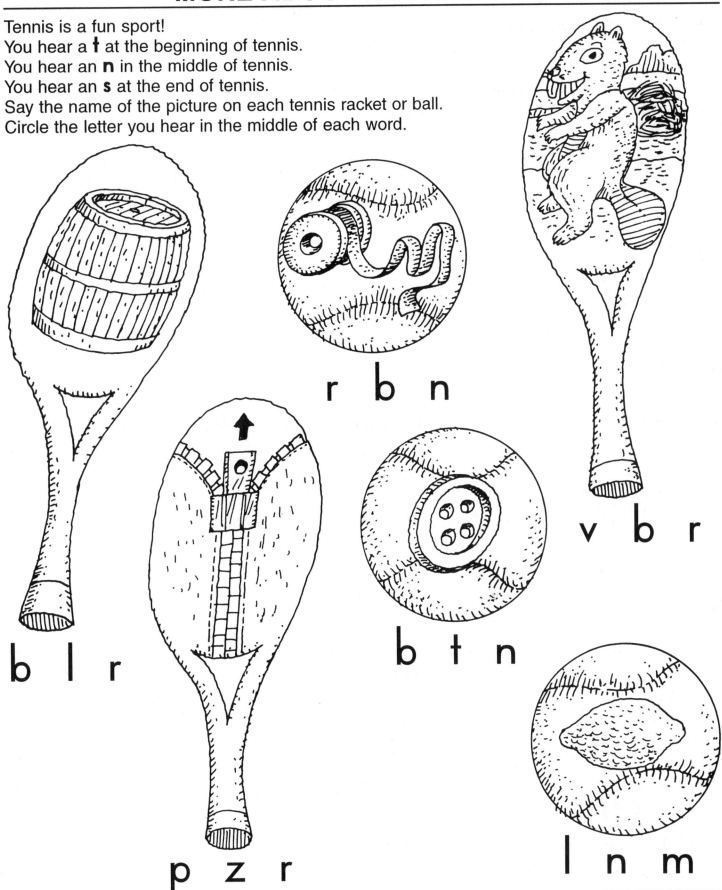

r b n

v b r

b l r

b t n

p z r

l n m

Skills: Auditory discrimination; Recognition of medial consonants; Sound/symbol association

MORE ABOUT CONSONANTS

We need to finish the puzzle.
You hear a **p** at the beginning of puzzle.
You hear a **z** in the middle of puzzle.
You hear an **l** at the end of puzzle.
Say the name of the picture on each puzzle piece.
Circle the letter you hear in the middle of each word.

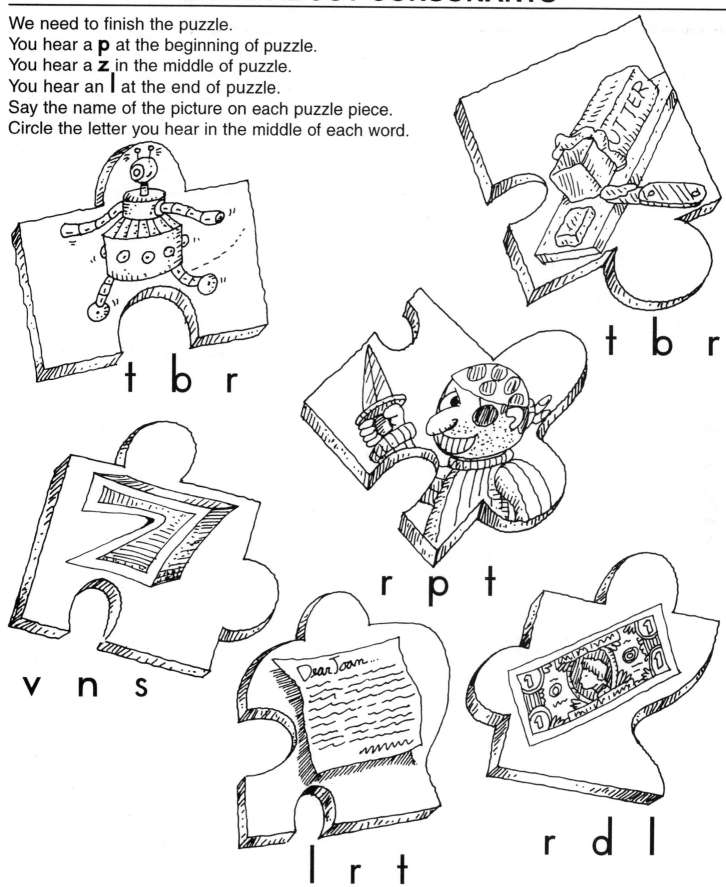

t b r

t b r

r p t

v n s

l r t

r d l

Skills: Auditory discrimination; Recognition of medial consonants; Sound/symbol association

MORE ABOUT CONSONANTS

Be careful not to step in a puddle!
You hear a **p** at the beginning of puddle.
You hear a **d** in the middle of puddle.
You hear an **l** at the end of puddle.
Say the name of the picture in each puddle.
Circle the letter you hear in the middle of each word.

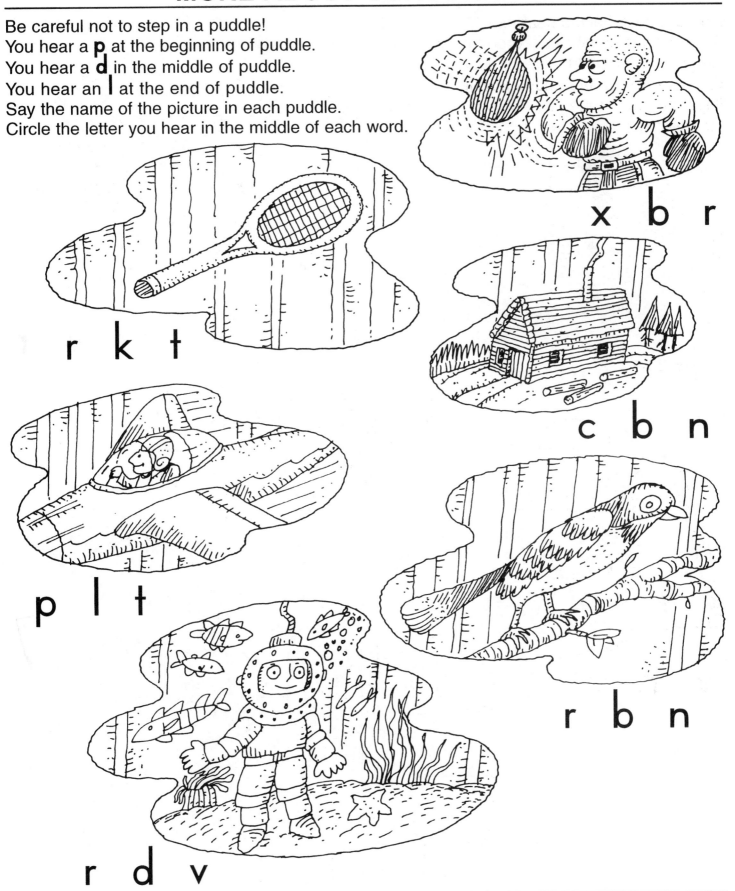

x b r

r k t

c b n

p l t

r b n

r d v

Skills: Auditory discrimination; Recognition of medial consonants; Sound/symbol association

MORE ABOUT CONSONANTS

Look at the picture in each box.
Write the letters whose sounds you hear at the beginning, middle, and end of each word.
Then color the picture.

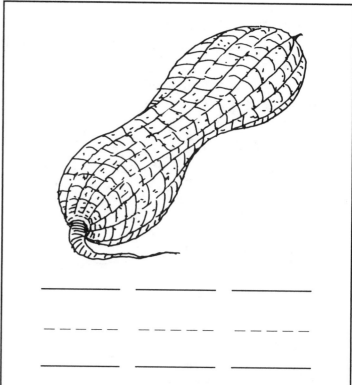

Skills: Recognition of consonants and their position in words; Fine motor skills; Auditory discrimination; Sound/symbol association

MORE ABOUT CONSONANTS

Look at the picture in each box.
Write the letters whose sounds you hear at the beginning, middle, and end of each word.
Then color the picture.

_____ _____ _____

- - - - - - - - - - - -

_____ _____ _____

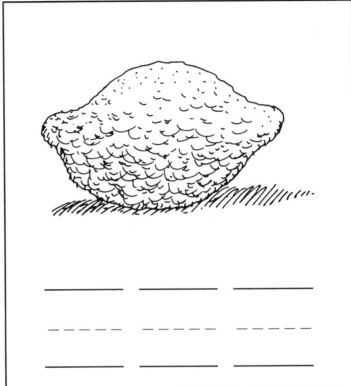

_____ _____ _____

- - - - - - - - - - - -

_____ _____ _____

_____ _____ _____

- - - - - - - - - - - -

_____ _____ _____

_____ _____ _____

- - - - - - - - - - - -

_____ _____ _____

Skills: Recognition of consonants and their position in words; Fine motor skills; Auditory discrimination; Sound/symbol association

MORE ABOUT CONSONANTS

Look at the picture in each box.
Write the letters whose sounds you hear at the beginning, middle, and end of each word.
Then color the picture.

_____ _____ _____

- - - - - - - - - - - -

_____ _____ _____

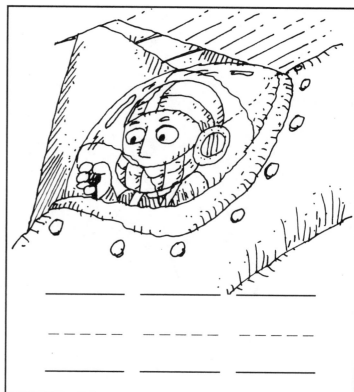

_____ _____ _____

- - - - - - - - - - - -

_____ _____ _____

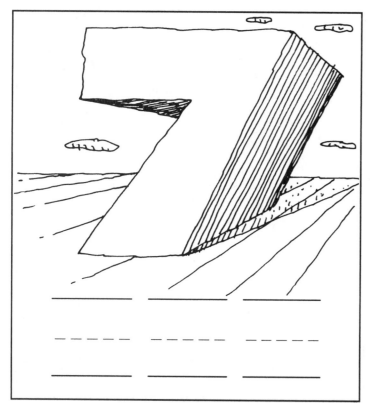

_____ _____ _____

- - - - - - - - - - - -

_____ _____ _____

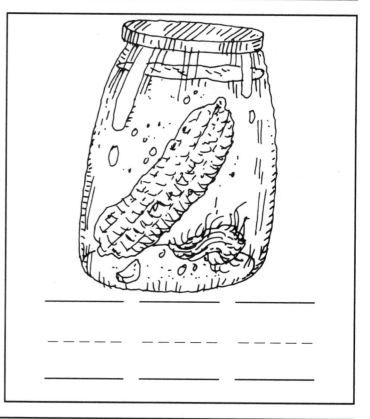

_____ _____ _____

- - - - - - - - - - - -

_____ _____ _____

Skills: Recognition of consonants and their position in words; Fine motor skills; Auditory discrimination; Sound/symbol association

MORE ABOUT CONSONANTS

Look at the picture in each box.
Write the letters whose sounds you hear at the beginning, middle, and end of each word.
Then color the picture.

_____ _____ _____

- - - - - - - - - - - - - - -

_____ _____ _____

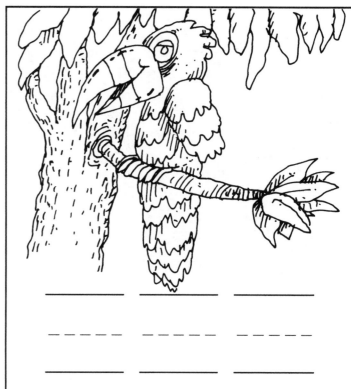

_____ _____ _____

- - - - - - - - - - - - - - -

_____ _____ _____

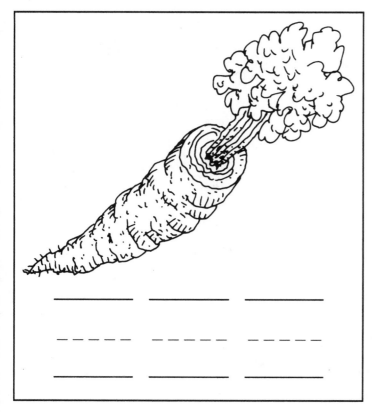

_____ _____ _____

- - - - - - - - - - - - - - -

_____ _____ _____

_____ _____ _____

- - - - - - - - - - - - - - -

_____ _____ _____

Skills: Recognition of consonants and their position in words; Fine motor skills; Auditory discrimination; Sound/symbol association

MORE ABOUT CONSONANTS

Look at the picture in each box.
Write the letters whose sounds you hear at the beginning, middle, and end of each word.
Then color the picture.

____ ____ ____

- - - -   - - - -   - - - -

____ ____ ____

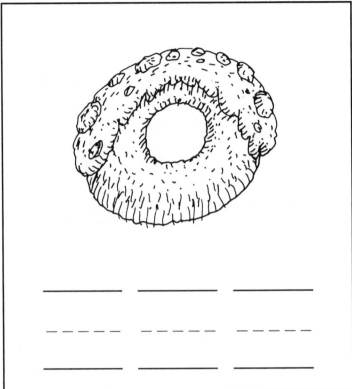

____ ____ ____

- - - -   - - - -   - - - -

____ ____ ____

- - - -   - - - -   - - - -

____ ____ ____

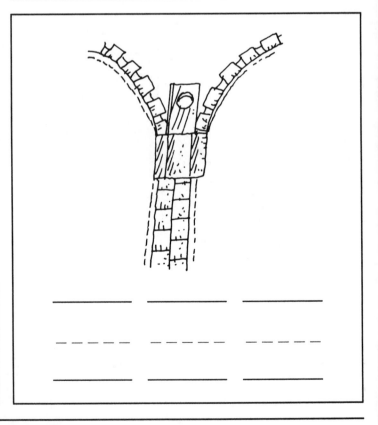

____ ____ ____

- - - -   - - - -   - - - -

Skills: Recognition of consonants and their position in words; Fine motor skills; Auditory discrimination; Sound/symbol association

130

MORE ABOUT CONSONANTS

Look at the picture in each box.
Write the letters whose sounds you hear at the beginning, middle, and end of each word.
Then color the picture.

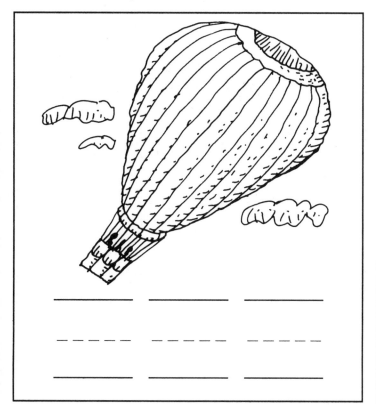

_____ _____ _____

- - - - - - - - - - - - - - - - -

_____ _____ _____

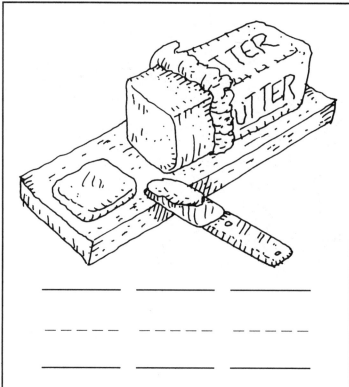

_____ _____ _____

- - - - - - - - - - - - - - - - -

_____ _____ _____

_____ _____ _____

- - - - - - - - - - - - - - - - -

_____ _____ _____

_____ _____ _____

- - - - - - - - - - - - - - - - -

_____ _____ _____

Skills: Recognition of consonants and their position in words; Fine motor skills; Auditory discrimination; Sound/symbol association

MORE ABOUT CONSONANTS

Look at the picture in each box.
Write the letters whose sounds you hear at the beginning, middle, and end of each word.
Then color the picture.

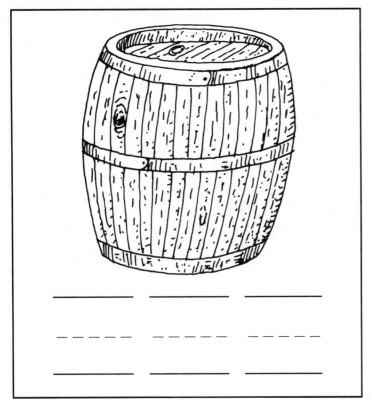

——— ——— ———

- - - - - - - - -

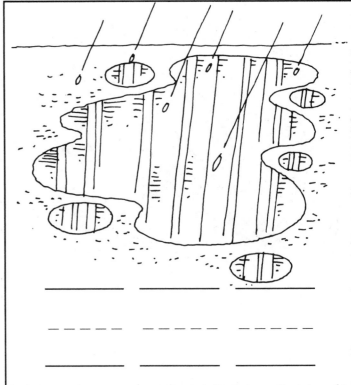

——— ——— ———

- - - - - - - - -

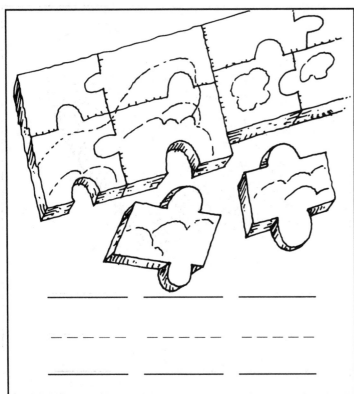

——— ——— ———

- - - - - - - - -

——— ——— ———

- - - - - - - - -

Skills: Recognition of consonants and their position in words; Fine motor skills; Auditory discrimination; Sound/symbol association

MORE ABOUT CONSONANTS

Look at the picture in each box.
Write the letters whose sounds you hear at the beginning, middle, and end of each word.
Then color the picture.

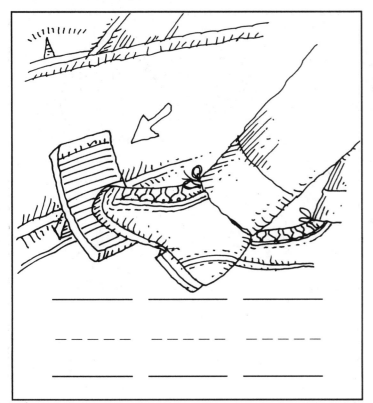

_____ _____ _____

_ _ _ _ _ _ _ _ _ _ _ _

_____ _____ _____

_____ _____ _____

_ _ _ _ _ _ _ _ _ _ _ _

_____ _____ _____

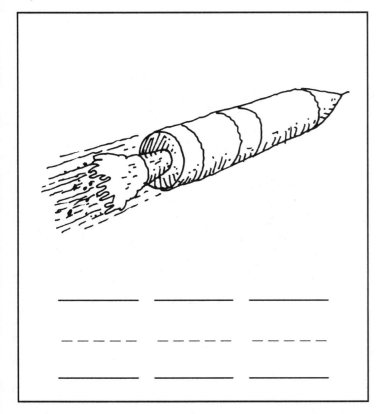

_____ _____ _____

_ _ _ _ _ _ _ _ _ _ _ _

_____ _____ _____

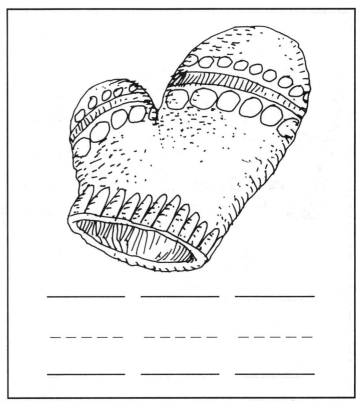

_____ _____ _____

_ _ _ _ _ _ _ _ _ _ _ _

_____ _____ _____

Skills: Recognition of consonants and their position in words; Fine motor skills; Auditory discrimination; Sound/symbol association

SHORT VOWELS

Look at the letter at the beginning of each row.
Look at the words in each row.
Circle the letter in each word where it appears.

a	cat	kite	pan	bug
e	pen	bed	box	pin
i	box	pig	bell	fish
o	bus	fan	sock	top
u	duck	gum	fox	bag

Skills: Recognition of the letters that are vowels; Association between letter symbols and words; Visual discrimination

SHORT VOWELS

Look at the letter at the beginning of each row.
Look at the words in each row.
Circle the letter in each word where it appears.

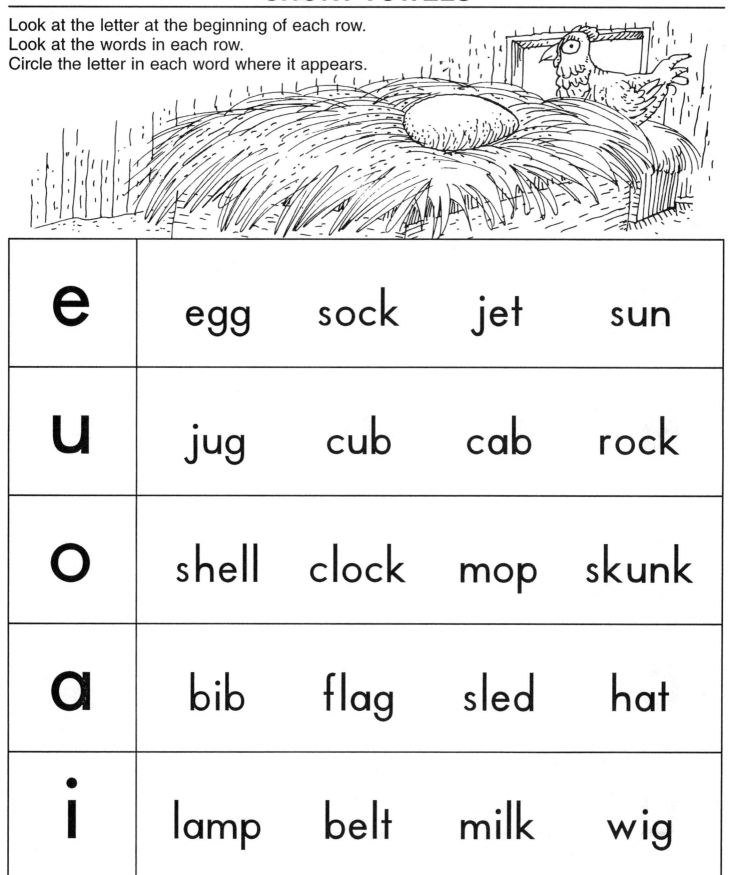

e	egg	sock	jet	sun
u	jug	cub	cab	rock
o	shell	clock	mop	skunk
a	bib	flag	sled	hat
i	lamp	belt	milk	wig

Skills: Recognition of the letters that are vowels; Association between letter symbols and words; Visual discrimination

SHORT VOWELS

Look at the word in each brick.
If the word has the vowel **a** in it, color the brick red.
If the word has the vowel **e** in it, color the brick blue.
If the word has the vowel **i** in it, color the brick green.
If the word has the vowel **o** in it, color the brick yellow.
If the word has the vowel **u** in it, color the brick orange.

Skills: Recognition of the letters that are vowels; Association between letter symbols and words; Visual discrimination

SHORT VOWELS

Look at the word in each pennant.
If the word has the vowel **a** in it, color the pennant red.
If the word has the vowel **e** in it, color the pennant blue.
If the word has the vowel **i** in it, color the pennant green.
If the word has the vowel **o** in it, color the pennant yellow.
If the word has the vowel **u** in it, color the pennant orange.

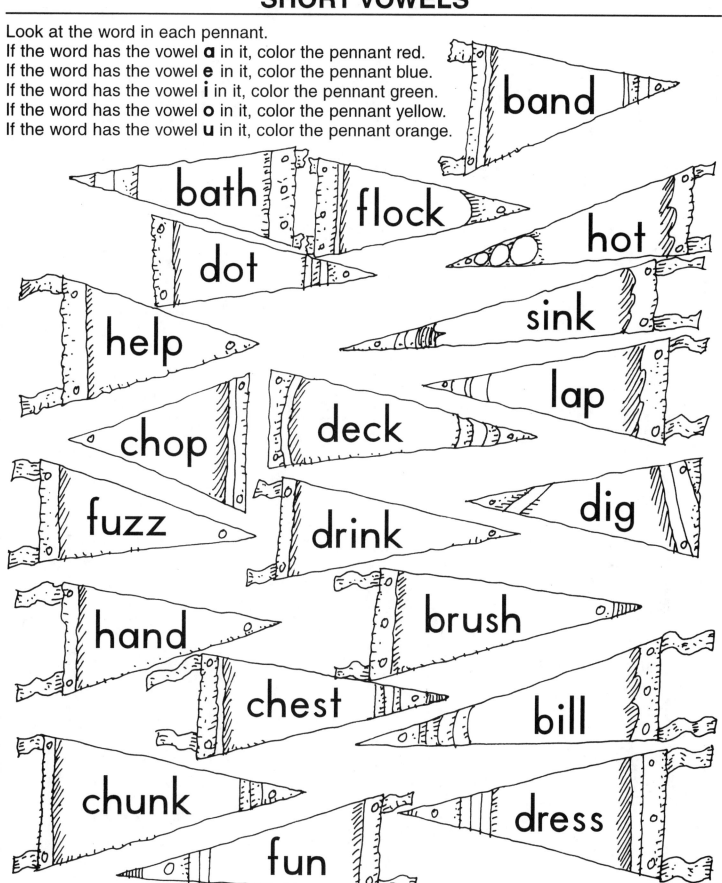

band

bath

flock

hot

dot

help

sink

chop

deck

lap

fuzz

drink

dig

hand

brush

chest

bill

chunk

dress

fun

Skills: Recognition of the letters that are vowels; Association between letter symbols and words; Visual discrimination

SHORT VOWELS

Look at the word in each sign.
If the word has the vowel **a** in it, color the sign red.
If the word has the vowel **e** in it, color the sign blue.
If the word has the vowel **i** in it, color the sign green.
If the word has the vowel **o** in it, color the sign yellow.
If the word has the vowel **u** in it, color the sign orange.

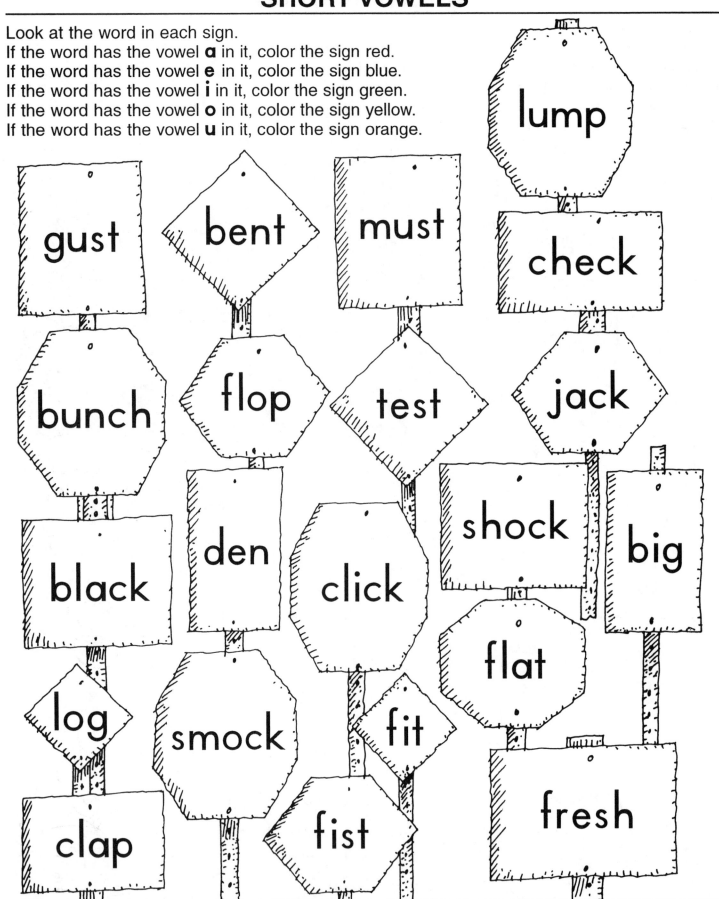

Skills: Recognition of the letters that are vowels; Association between letter symbols and words; Visual discrimination

SHORT VOWELS

Short vowel: ă

The vowel **a** makes the sound you hear in apple.
Look at the apples on the tree.
Color the apples that have pictures with the short **a** sound.

Skills: Recognition of the short vowel "a"; Auditory discrimination

SHORT VOWELS

Short vowel: ĕ

The vowel **e** makes the sound you hear in egg.
Look at the eggs.
Color the eggs that have pictures with the short **e** sound.

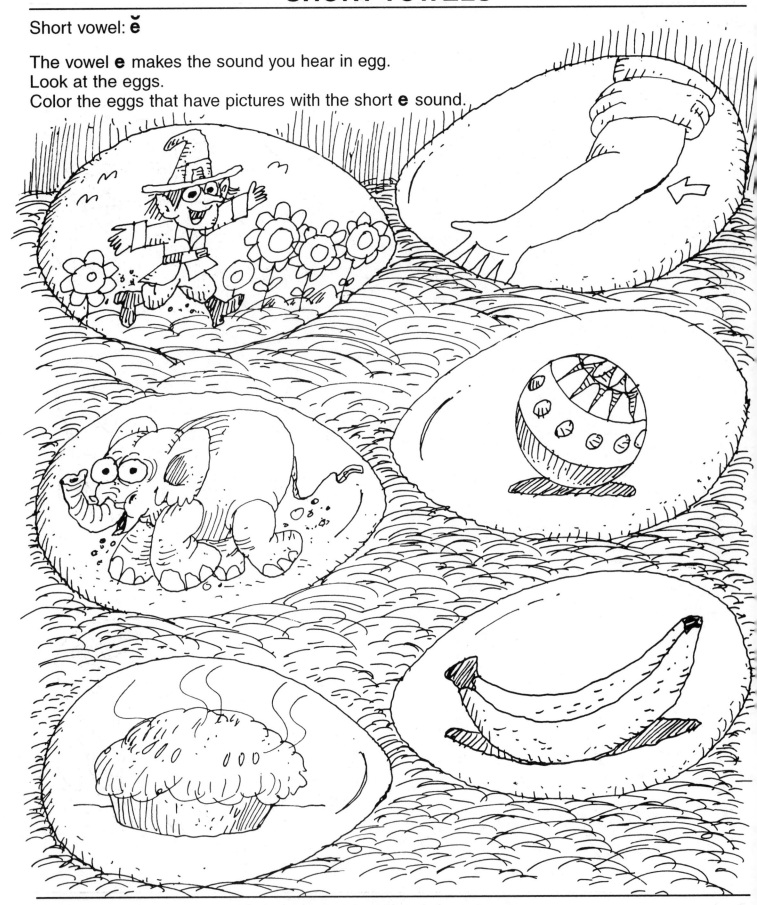

Skills: Recognition of the short vowel "e"; Auditory discrimination

SHORT VOWELS

Short vowel: ĭ

The vowel **i** makes the sound you hear in insect.
Look at the insects on this page.
Color the insects that have pictures with the short **i** sound.

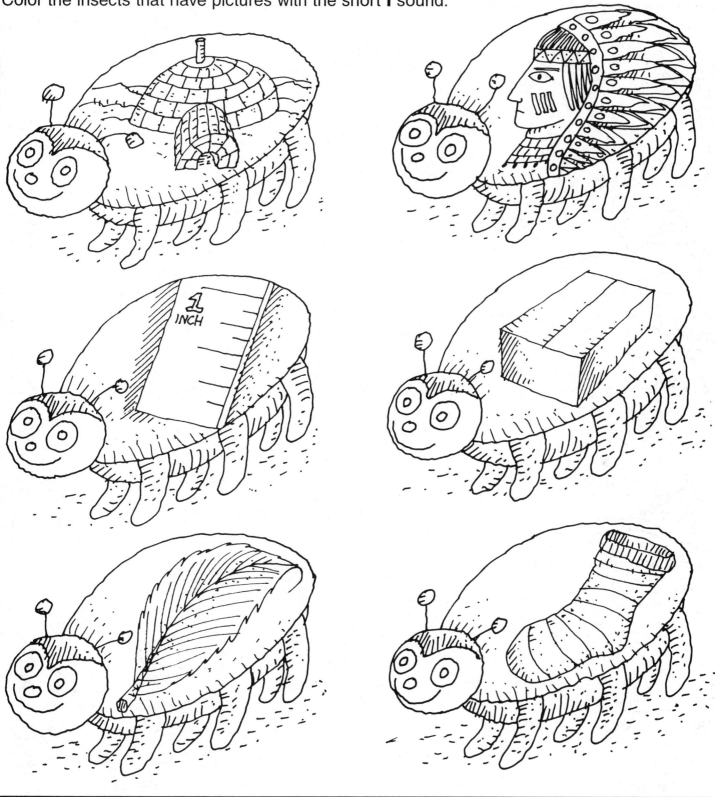

Skills: Recognition of the short vowel "i"; Auditory discrimination

SHORT VOWELS

Short vowel: ŏ

The vowel **o** makes the sound you hear in otter.
Look at the otters playing in the water.
Color the otters that have pictures with the short **o** sound.

Skills: Recognition of the short vowel "o"; Auditory discrimination

SHORT VOWELS

Short vowel: ŭ

The vowel **u** makes the sound you hear in umbrella.
Look at the umbrellas on this page.
Color the umbrellas that have pictures with the short **u** sound.

Skills: Recognition of the short vowel "u"; Auditory discrimination

SHORT VOWELS

Short vowel: ă

Listen to the short **a** sound you hear in cat.
Look at the pictures on this page.
Draw lines from the pictures whose names have the short **a** sound to the cat.

Skills: Recognition of the short vowel "a"; Auditory discrimination

SHORT VOWELS

Short vowel: ĕ

Listen to the short **e** sound you hear in bell.
Look at the pictures on this page.
Draw lines from the pictures whose names have the short **e** sound to the bell.

Skills: Recognition of the short vowel "e"; Auditory discrimination

SHORT VOWELS

Short vowel: ĭ

Listen to the short **i** sound you hear in pig.
Look at the pictures on this page.
Draw lines from the pictures whose names have the short **i** sound to the pig.

Skills: Recognition of the short vowel "i"; Auditory discrimination

SHORT VOWELS

Short vowel: ŏ

Listen to the short **o** sound you hear in fox.
Look at the pictures on this page.
Draw lines from the pictures whose names have the short **o** sound to the fox.

Skills: Recognition of the short vowel "o"; Auditory discrimination

SHORT VOWELS

Short vowel: ŭ

Listen to the short **u** sound you hear in bug.
Look at the pictures on this page.
Draw lines from the pictures whose names have the short **u** sound to the bug.

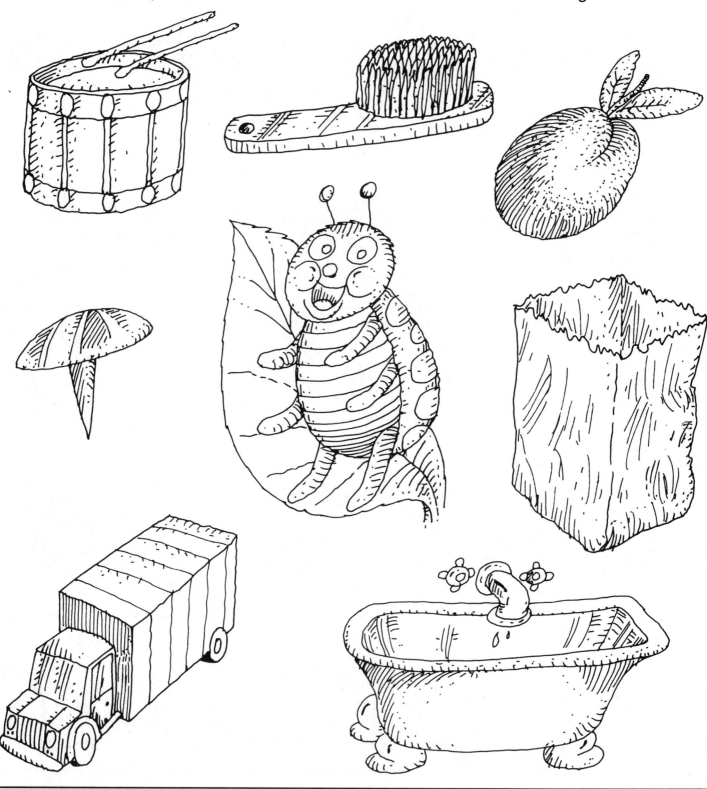

Skills: Recognition of the short vowel "u"; Auditory discrimination

SHORT VOWELS

Look at the vowel at the beginning of each row.
Think about the short vowel sound it makes.
Look at the pictures in each row.
Circle the pictures whose names contain that short vowel sound.

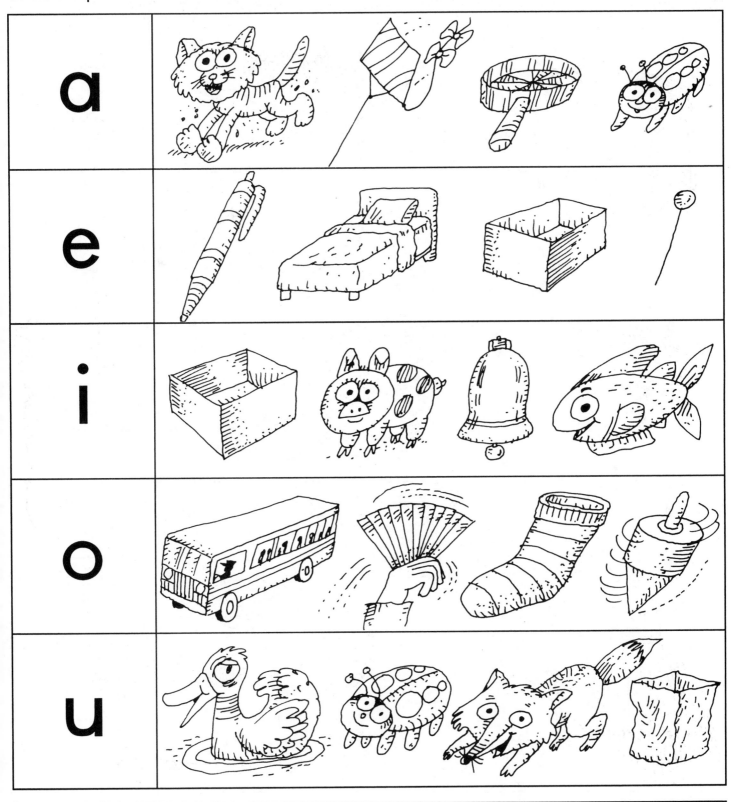

Skills: Recognition of the letters that are vowels; Association between sounds, symbols, and words; Visual discrimination

SHORT VOWELS

Look at the vowel at the beginning of each row.
Think about the short vowel sound it makes.
Look at the pictures in each row.
Circle the pictures whose names contain that short vowel sound.

Skills: Recognition of the letters that are vowels; Association between sounds, symbols, and words; Visual discrimination

SHORT VOWELS

Look who is in each wagon.
Look at the letters under each picture.
What sound is missing?
Write the missing vowel to finish the word.

Skills: Recognition of short vowels; Writing letters and words; Association between sounds, symbols, and words

SHORT VOWELS

Look what is on each wagon.
Look at the letters under each picture.
What sound is missing?
Write the missing vowel to finish the word.

d __ ll

s __ d

h __ t

m __ tt

dr __ m

Skills: Recognition of short vowels; Writing letters and words; Association between sounds, symbols, and words

SHORT VOWELS

Look at the picture in each box.
Look at the words next to each picture.
Circle the word that names the picture.
Then color the pictures.

pen	cup	big
pin	cop	bug
pan	cap	bag
lick	stick	black
lock	stack	block
luck	stuck	blink
limp	desk	swing
lump	dusk	swung
lamp	disk	swam

Skills: Recognizing short vowel sounds; Association between sounds, symbols, and words

SHORT VOWELS

Look at the first picture in each row.
Look at the rest of the pictures in that row.
Circle the picture that has the same vowel sound as the first picture.

Skills: Recognizing short vowel sounds; Comparing sounds that are alike; Auditory discrimination

SHORT VOWELS

Look at the first picture in each row.
Look at the rest of the pictures in that row.
Circle the picture that has the same vowel sound as the first picture.

Skills: Recognizing short vowel sounds; Comparing sounds that are alike; Auditory discrimination

LONG VOWELS

Long vowel: ā

Frame has a long **a** sound.
Look at the picture in each frame.
Color the pictures that have the long **a** sound.

Skills: Recognition of the long vowel "a"; Association between sounds and symbols; Auditory discrimination

LONG VOWELS

Long vowel: $\bar{e}$

Peach has a long **e** sound.
Look at the picture in each peach.
Color the pictures that have the long **e** sound.

Skills: Recognition of the long vowel "e"; Association between sounds and symbols; Auditory discrimination

LONG VOWELS

Long vowel: $\bar{i}$

Kite has a long **i** sound.
Look at the picture in each kite.
Color the pictures that have the long **i** sound.

Skills: Recognition of the long vowel "i"; Association between sounds and symbols; Auditory discrimination

LONG VOWELS

Long vowel: ō

Soap has a long **o** sound.
Look at the picture on each bar of soap.
Color the pictures that have the long **o** sound.

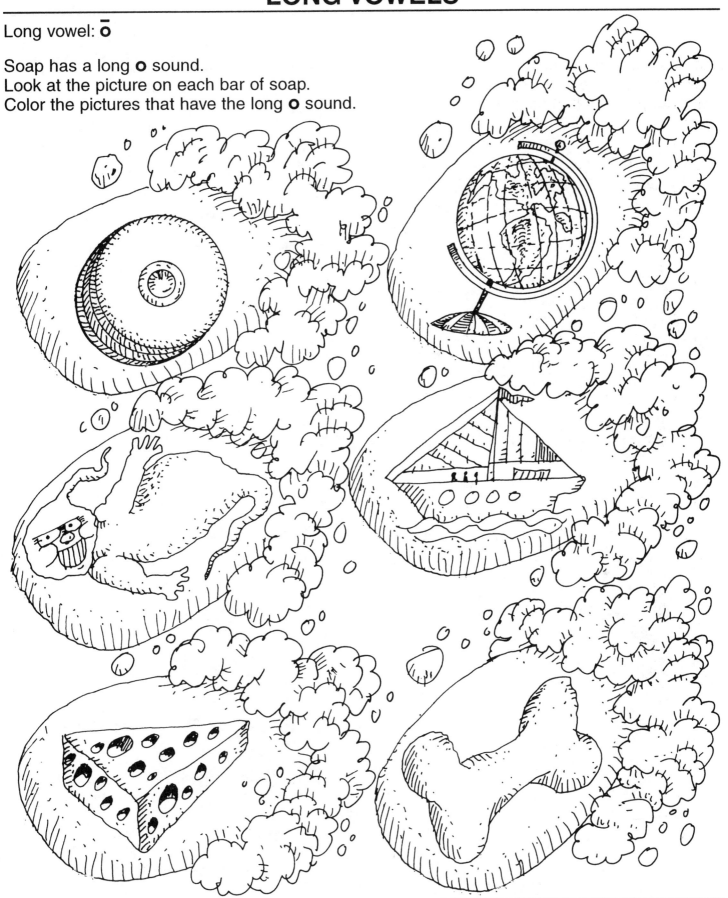

Skills: Recognition of the long vowel "o"; Association between sounds and symbols; Auditory discrimination

LONG VOWELS

Long vowel: **ū**

Cube has a long **u** sound.
Look at the picture in each ice cube.
Color the pictures that have the long **u** sound.

Skills: Recognition of the long vowel "u"; Association between sounds and symbols; Auditory discrimination

LONG VOWELS

Look at the words on the left.
Look at the pictures on the right.
Draw a line to match each word to the correct picture.

cap

cape

kite

kiss

Skills: Recognition of short and long vowel sounds; Matching pictures and words;
Association between sounds, symbols, and words

LONG VOWELS

Look at the words on the left.
Look at the pictures on the right.
Draw a line to match each word to the correct picture.

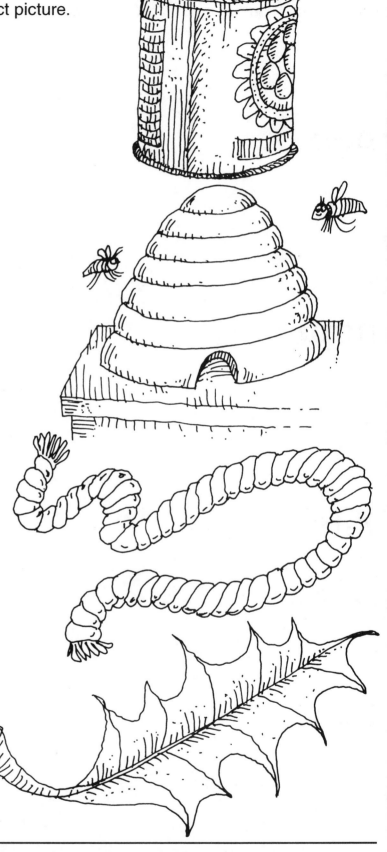

hive

leaf

can

rope

Skills: Recognition of short and long vowel sounds; Matching pictures and words;
Association between sounds, symbols, and words

LONG VOWELS

Look at the words on the left.
Look at the pictures on the right.
Draw a line to match each word to the correct picture.

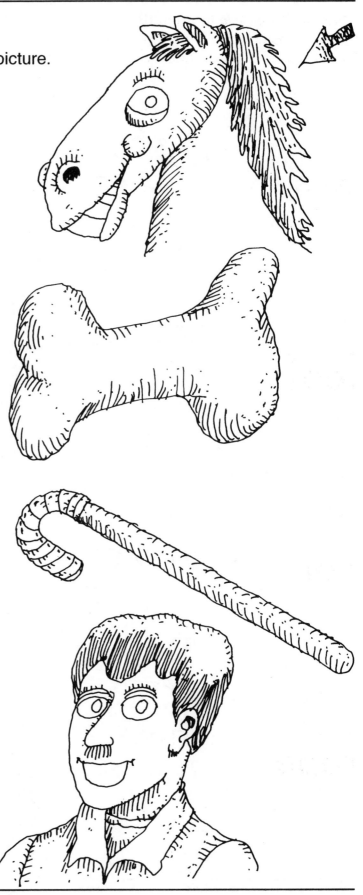

bone

mane

man

cane

Skills: Recognition of short and long vowel sounds; Matching pictures and words;
Association between sounds, symbols, and words

LONG VOWELS

Look at the words in each flag.
Color all the parts of the flags that contain words with long vowel sounds.

cat
cane
hat

bite
bit
ride

snake
pan
hive

nine
wig
tire

Skills: Recognition of short and long vowel sounds; Association between sounds, symbols, and words

LONG VOWELS

Look at the words in each flag.
Color all the parts of the flags that contain words with long vowel sounds.

prize

cat

bell

cone

sled

leaf

cake

lake

bed

well

pin

boat

Skills: Recognition of short and long vowel sounds; Association between sounds, symbols, and words

LONG VOWELS

Look at the words in the box at the top of the page.
Look at the picture in each box.
Write a word from the box under the matching picture.

pail	coat	hive	cake

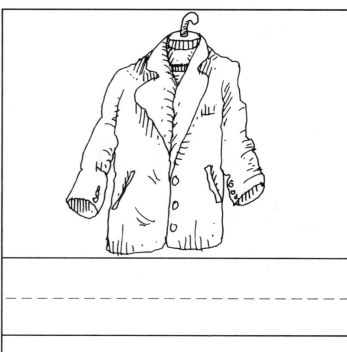

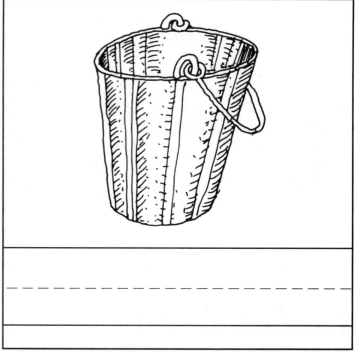

Skills: Recognition of long vowel sounds; Writing letters and words; Association between sounds, symbols, and words

LONG VOWELS

Look at the words in the box at the top of the page.
Look at the picture in each box.
Write a word from the box under the matching picture.

| feet | tube | flute | dive |

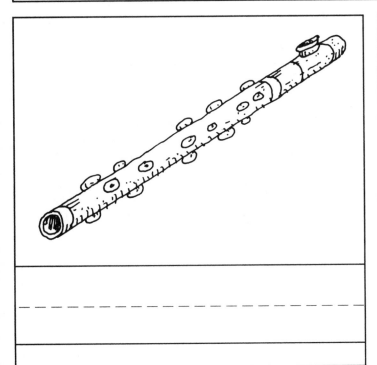

_____

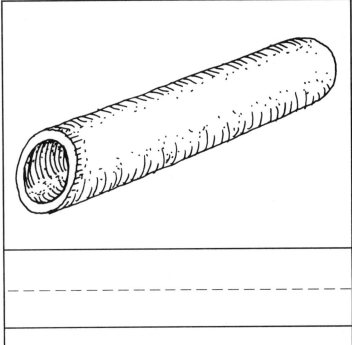

_____

_____

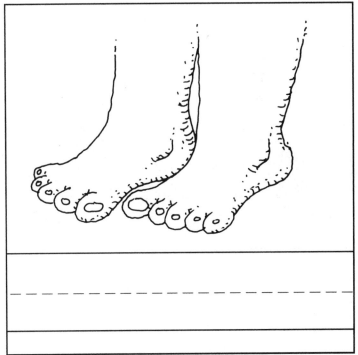

_____

Skills: Recognition of long vowel sounds; Writing letters and words; Association between sounds, symbols, and words

LONG VOWELS

Look at the words in the box at the top of the page.
Look at the picture in each box.
Write a word from the box under the matching picture.

seal	rose	rake	goat

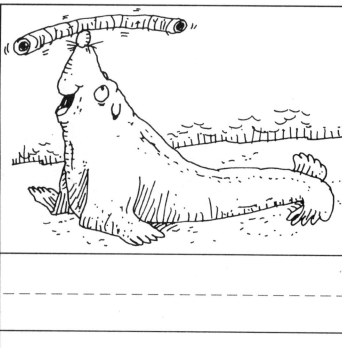

Skills: Recognition of long vowel sounds; Writing letters and words; Association between sounds, symbols, and words

LONG VOWELS

Look at the words in the box at the top of the page.
Look at the picture in each box.
Write a word from the box under the matching picture.

fire	nest	tie	road

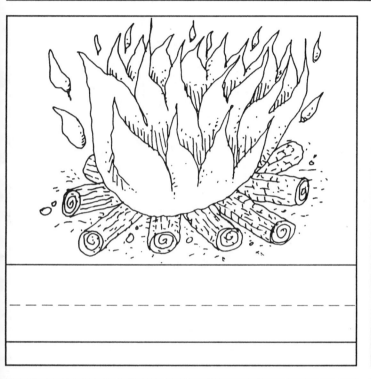

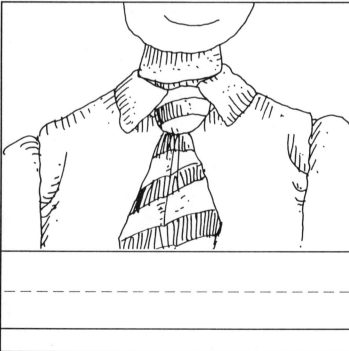

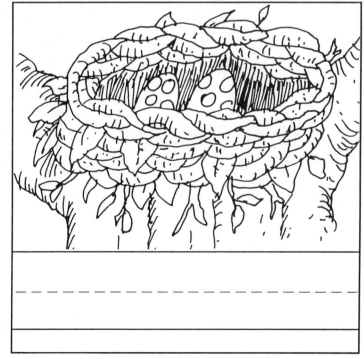

Skills: Recognition of long and short vowel sounds; Writing letters and words; Association between sounds, symbols, and words

LONG VOWELS

Look at the words in the box at the top of the page.
Look at the picture in each box.
Write a word from the box under the matching picture.

bed	nine	lamp	bead

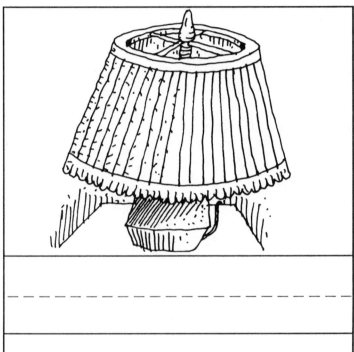

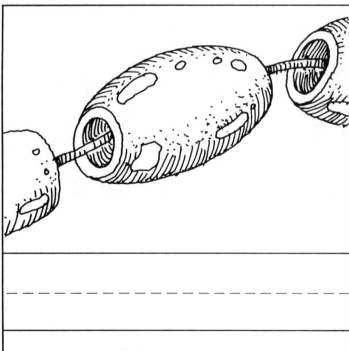

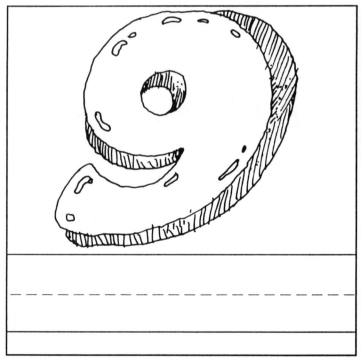

Skills: Recognition of long and short vowel sounds; Writing letters and words; Association between sounds, symbols, and words

LONG VOWELS

Look at the words in the box at the top of the page.
Look at the picture in each box.
Write a word from the box under the matching picture.

top	mail	jeep	globe

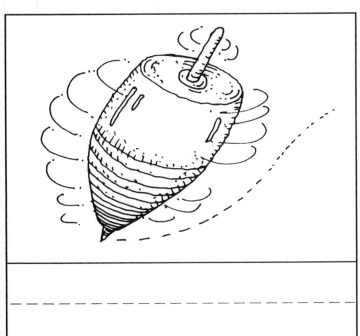

Skills: Recognition of long and short vowel sounds; Writing letters and words; Association between sounds, symbols, and words

LONG VOWELS

The long **a** sound can be spelled in several ways.
Think about the **a_e** in cake, the **ai** in rain and the **ay** in play.
Look at the picture and word in each box.
Circle the letters that make the long **a** sound in each word.
Then color the pictures.

cape

paint

hay

cave

Skills: Identifying the long vowel "a" spelled in various ways; Association between sounds, symbols, and words

LONG VOWELS

The long **a** sound can be spelled in several ways.
Think about the **a_e** in cake, the **ai** in rain and the **ay** in play.
Look at the picture and word in each box.
Circle the letters that make the long **a** sound in each word.
Then color the pictures.

plane

nail

jay

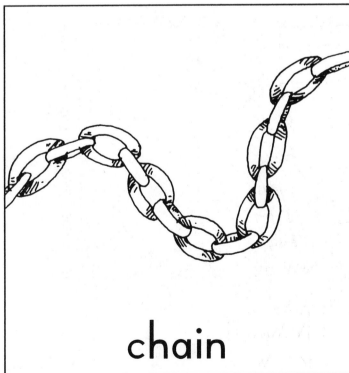

chain

Skills: Identifying the long vowel "a" spelled in various ways; Association between sounds, symbols, and words

LONG VOWELS

The long **e** sound can be spelled in several ways.
Think about the **ee** in feet and the **ea** in leaf.
Look at the picture and word in each box.
Circle the letters that make the long **e** sound in each word.
Then color the pictures.

tree

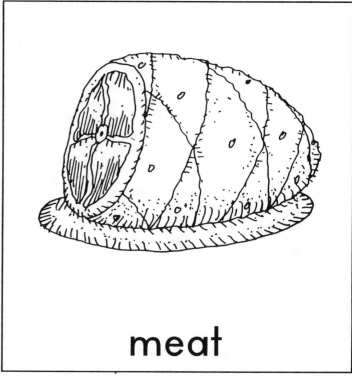

meat

seal

queen

Skills: Identifying the long vowel "e" spelled in various ways; Association between sounds, symbols, and words

LONG VOWELS

The long **e** sound can be spelled in several ways.
Think about the **ee** in feet and the **ea** in leaf.
Look at the picture and word in each box.
Circle the letters that make the long **e** sound in each word.
Then color the pictures.

peach

beet

sheep

read

Skills: Identifying the long vowel "e" spelled in various ways; Association between sounds, symbols, and words

LONG VOWELS

The long **i** sound can be spelled in several ways.
Think about the **i_e** in hive and the **ie** in lie.
Look at the picture and word in each box.
Circle the letters that make the long **i** sound in each word.
Then color the pictures.

bike

pie

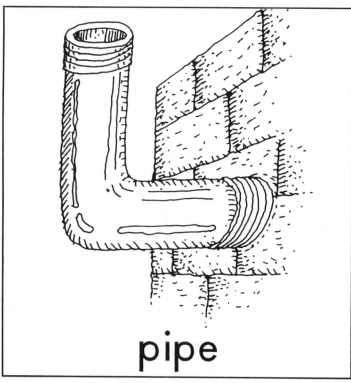

pipe

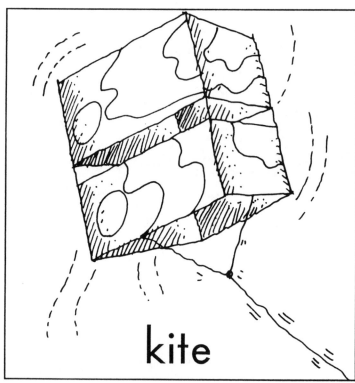

kite

Skills: Identifying the long vowel "i" spelled in various ways; Association between sounds, symbols, and words

LONG VOWELS

The long **i** sound can be spelled in several ways.
Think about the **i_e** in hive and the **ie** in lie.
Look at the picture and word in each box.
Circle the letters that make the long **i** sound in each word.
Then color the pictures.

tie

dime

lime

flies

Skills: Identifying the long vowel "i" spelled in various ways; Association between sounds, symbols, and words

LONG VOWELS

The long **o** sound can be spelled in several ways.
Think about the **o_e** in rose, the **oa** in road, and the **ow** in row.
Look at the picture and word in each box.
Circle the letters that make the long **o** sound in each word.
Then color the pictures.

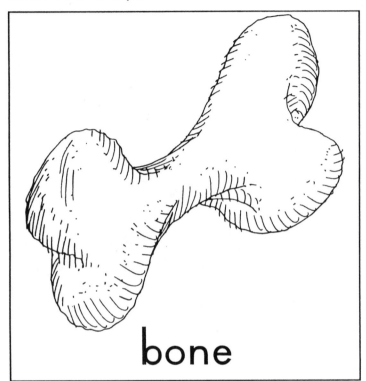

bone

soap

mow

globe

Skills: Identifying the long vowel "o" spelled in various ways; Association between sounds, symbols, and words

178

LONG VOWELS

The long **o** sound can be spelled in several ways.
Think about the **o_e** in rose, the **oa** in road, and the **ow** in row.
Look at the picture and word in each box.
Circle the letters that make the long **o** sound in each word.
Then color the pictures.

boat

goat

snow

rose

Skills: Identifying the long vowel "o" spelled in various ways; Association between sounds, symbols, and words

LONG VOWELS

The long **u** sound can be spelled in several ways.
Think about the **u_e** in cute and the **ue** in true.
Look at the picture and word in each box.
Circle the letters that make the long **u** sound in each word.
Then color the pictures.

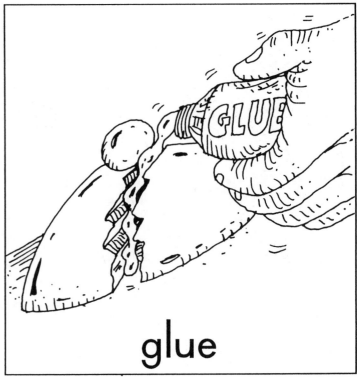

cube

glue

tune

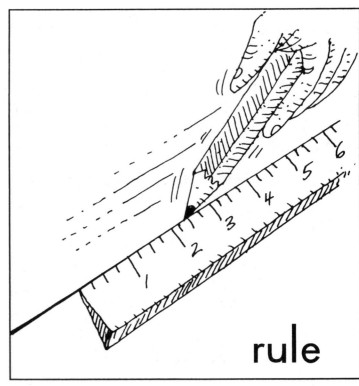

rule

Skills: Identifying the long vowel "u" spelled in various ways; Association between sounds, symbols, and words

LONG VOWELS

The long **u** sound can be spelled in several ways.
Think about the **u_e** in cute and the **ue** in true.
Look at the picture and word in each box.
Circle the letters that make the long **u** sound in each word.
Then color the pictures.

mule

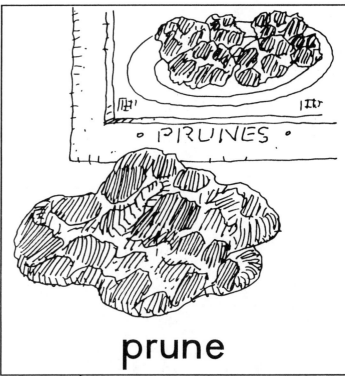

prune

blue

flute

Skills: Identifying the long vowel "u" spelled in various ways; Association between sounds, symbols, and words

LONG VOWELS

Look at the vowels at the top of the page.
Look at the letters in each box.
Fill in the missing vowel to make a word.
Then draw a picture to show the word you made.

a	e	i	o	u

b _ ne

c _ ke

pl _ ne

k _ te

Skills: Recognizing long vowel sounds; Writing words and letters; Association between sounds, symbols, and words

LONG VOWELS

Look at the vowels at the top of the page.
Look at the letters in each box.
Fill in the missing vowel to make a word.
Then draw a picture to show the word you made.

a	e	i	o	u

c __ ne

b __ ke

g __ me

c __ be

Skills: Recognizing long vowel sounds; Writing words and letters; Association between sounds, symbols, and words

LONG VOWELS

Look at the vowels at the top of the page.
Look at the letters in each box.
Fill in the missing vowel to make a word.
Then draw a picture to show the word you made.

a   e   i   o   u

t __ be

n __ se

pl __ te

g __ te

Skills: Recognizing long vowel sounds; Writing words and letters; Association between sounds, symbols, and words

LONG VOWELS

Look at the picture in each box.
Look at the letters in each box.
Fill in the missing vowels to make a word.

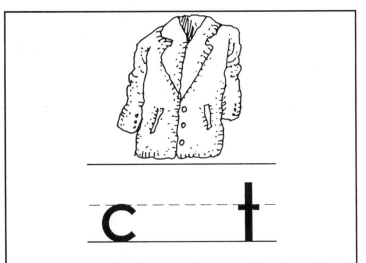

c   t

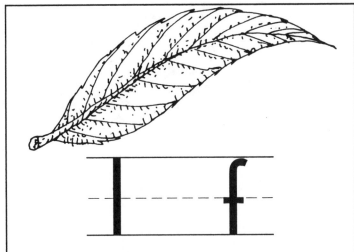

l   f

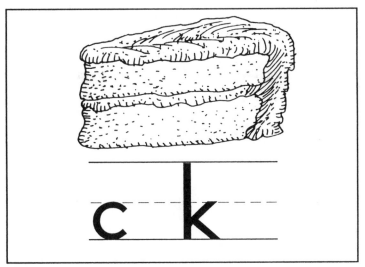

c   k

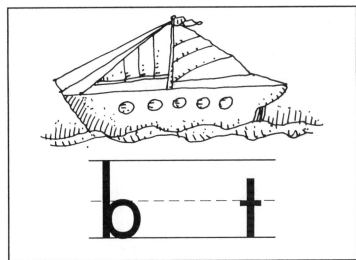

b   t

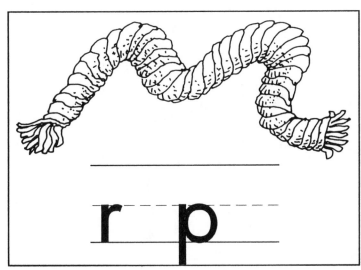

r   p

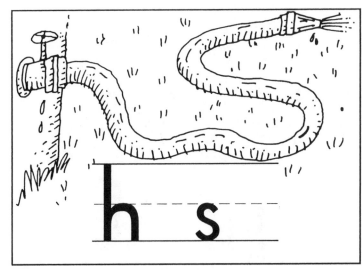

h   s

Skills: Recognizing long vowel sounds; Writing words and letters; Association between sounds, symbols, and words

LONG VOWELS

Look at the picture in each box.
Look at the letters in each box.
Fill in the missing vowels to make a word.

c ___ n

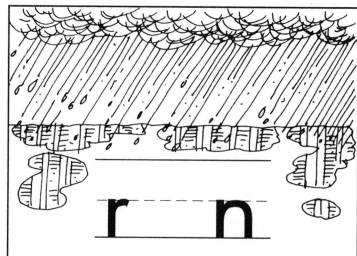

r ___ ___ n

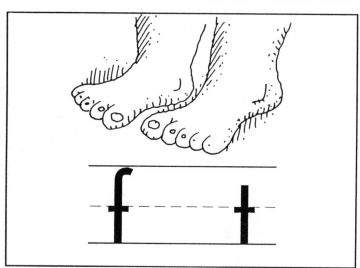

f ___ ___ t

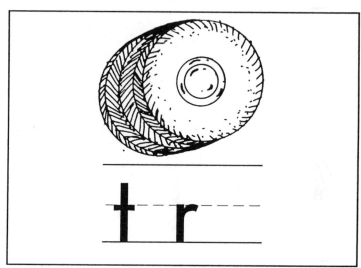

t ___ r ___

g ___ ___ t

s l ___ d ___

Skills: Recognizing long vowel sounds; Writing words and letters; Association between sounds, symbols, and words

LONG VOWELS

Look at the picture in each box.
Look at the words in each box.
Circle the word that matches the picture.

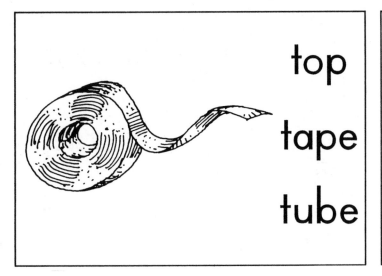

top

tape

tube

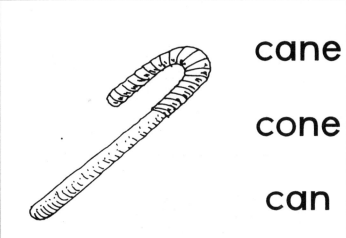

cane

cone

can

bead

band

bed

sap

sip

soap

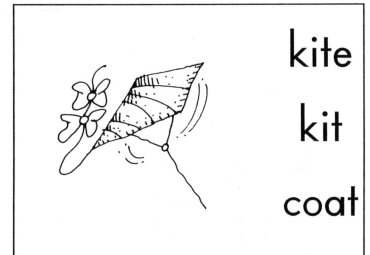

kite

kit

coat

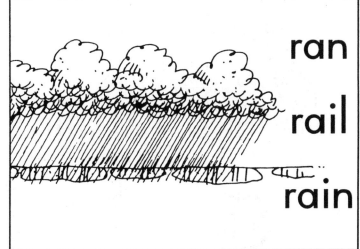

ran

rail

rain

Skills: Recognizing short and long vowel sounds; Association between sounds, symbols, and words

LONG VOWELS

Look at the picture in each box.
Look at the words in each box.
Circle the word that matches the picture.

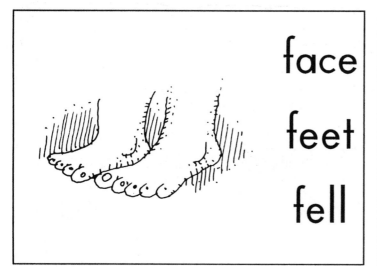

face

feet

fell

gate

grip

goat

boat

band

beet

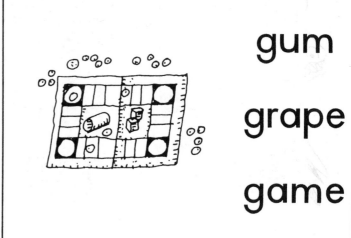

gum

grape

game

pine

pin

pen

cap

cave

cape

Skills: Recognizing short and long vowel sounds; Association between sounds, symbols, and words

COMBINING CONSONANTS

Look at the picture at the top of each column.
Look at the pictures underneath it.
Color the pictures whose names begin with the same sound.

Skills: Understanding that some consonants can be blended together; Sound/symbol association

COMBINING CONSONANTS

Look at the picture at the top of each column.
Look at the pictures underneath it.
Color the pictures whose names begin with the same sound.

Skills: Understanding that some consonants can be blended together; Sound/symbol association

COMBINING CONSONANTS

Look at the picture at the top of each column.
Look at the pictures underneath it.
Color the pictures whose names begin with the same sound.

Skills: Understanding that some consonants can be blended together; Sound/symbol association

COMBINING CONSONANTS

Look at the picture at the top of each column.
Look at the pictures underneath it.
Color the pictures whose names begin with the same sound.

Skills: Understanding that some consonants can be blended together; Sound/symbol association

COMBINING CONSONANTS

Look at the first picture in each row.
Its name begins with **st**, **sp**, **sl**, or **sk**.
Look at the rest of the pictures in each row.
Circle the pictures whose names begin with the same sound.

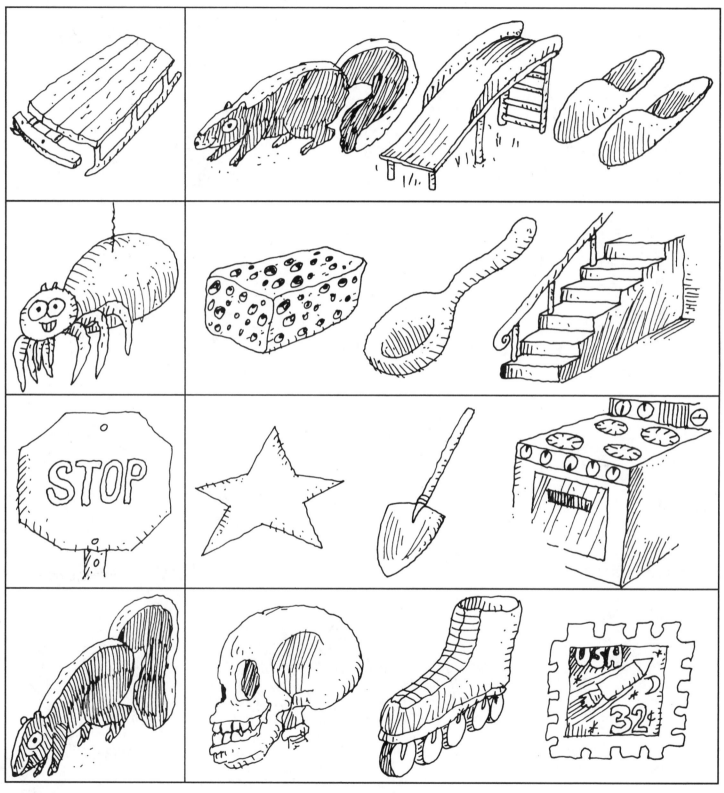

Skills: Understanding that some consonants can be blended together; Sound/symbol association

COMBINING CONSONANTS

Look at the first picture in each row.
Its name begins with **str**, **spr**, **scr**, or **squ**.
Look at the rest of the pictures in each row.
Circle the picture whose name begins with the same sound.

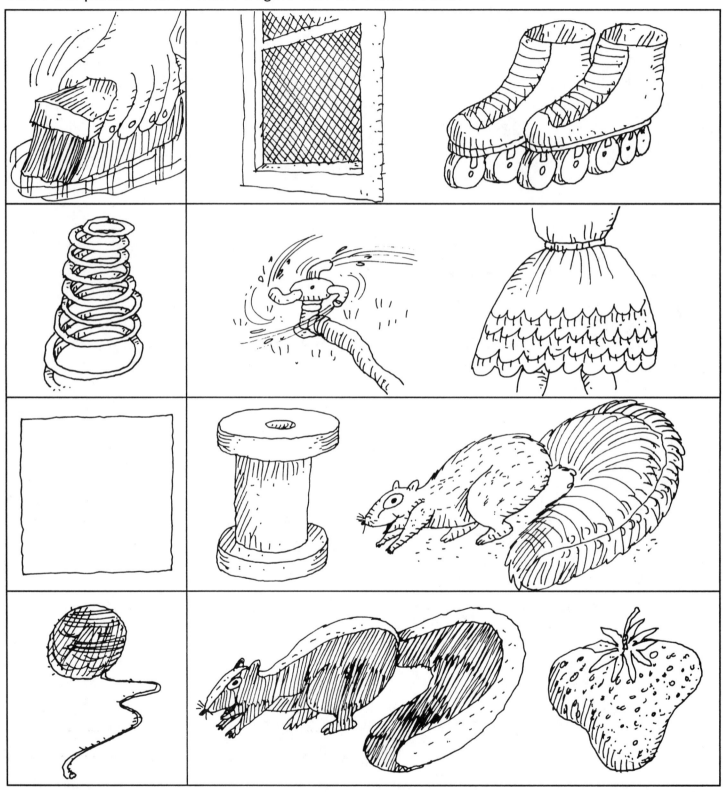

Skills: Understanding that some consonants can be blended together; Sound/symbol association

194

COMBINING CONSONANTS

Look at the first picture in each row.
Its name begins with **sm**, **sn**, **sw**, or **sc**.
Look at the rest of the pictures in each row.
Circle the pictures whose names begin with the same sound.

Skills: Understanding that some consonants can be blended together; Sound/symbol association

COMBINING CONSONANTS

Look at the consonant blends on the left.
Look at the pictures on the right and say their names.
Draw a line to match the consonant blend with the sound you hear
at the beginning of each word.

pr

br

dr

fr

Skills: Understanding that some consonants can be blended together; Sound/symbol
association

COMBINING CONSONANTS

Look at the consonant blends on the left.
Look at the pictures on the right and say their names.
Draw a line to match the consonant blend with the sound you hear
at the beginning of each word.

cl

fl

gl

bl

Skills: Understanding that some consonants can be blended together; Sound/symbol
association

COMBINING CONSONANTS

Look at the consonant blends on the left.
Look at the pictures on the right and say their names.
Draw a line to match the consonant blend with the sound you hear
at the beginning of each word.

gl

pl

bl

fl

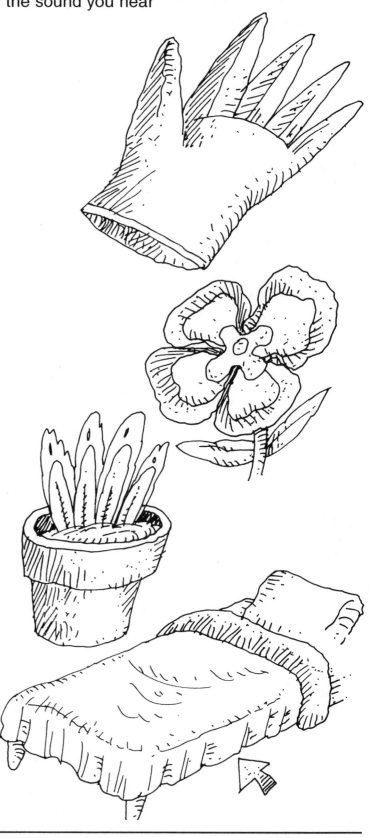

Skills: Understanding that some consonants can be blended together; Sound/symbol
association

COMBINING CONSONANTS

Look at the consonant blends on the left.
Look at the pictures on the right and say their names.
Draw a line to match the consonant blend with the sound you hear
at the beginning of each word.

sk

st

sl

sp

Skills: Understanding that some consonants can be blended together; Sound/symbol
association

COMBINING CONSONANTS

Look at the consonant blends on the left.
Look at the pictures on the right and say their names.
Draw a line to match the consonant blend with the sound you hear
at the beginning of each word.

squ

str

spr

scr

Skills: Understanding that some consonants can be blended together; Sound/symbol
association

COMBINING CONSONANTS

Look at the consonant blends on the left.
Look at the pictures on the right and say their names.
Draw a line to match the consonant blend with the sound you hear
at the beginning of each word.

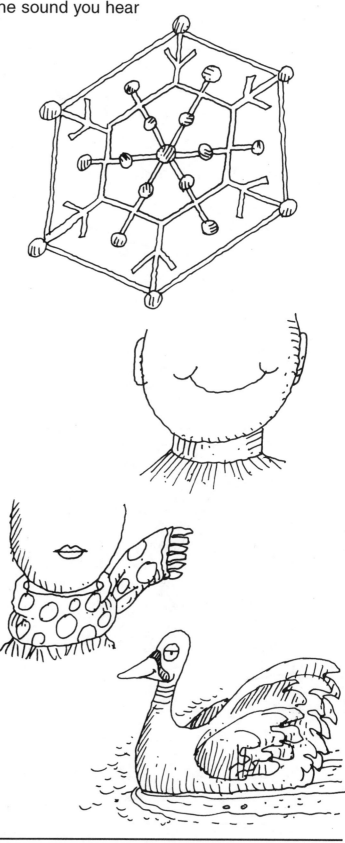

sm

sc

sw

sn

Skills: Understanding that some consonants can be blended together; Sound/symbol
association

COMBINING CONSONANTS

Look at the picture in each box.
Look at the letters in each box.
Write the blend that you hear at the beginning of each pictured word.
Then color the pictures.

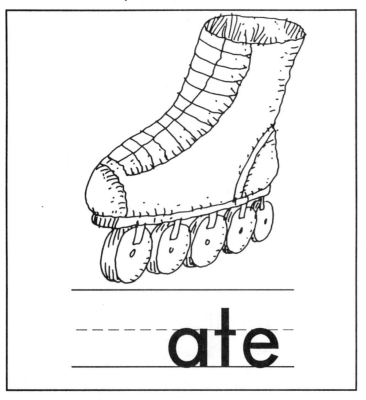

_ _ _ _ _ **ate**

_ _ _ _ _ **ed**

_ _ _ _ _ **een**

_ _ _ _ _ **ail**

Skills: Recognizing consonant blends; Sound/symbol association; Writing words and letters

COMBINING CONSONANTS

Look at the picture in each box.
Look at the letters in each box.
Write the blend that you hear at the beginning of each pictured word.
Then color the pictures.

_____**um**

_____**obe**

_____**im**

_____**ock**

Skills: Recognizing consonant blends; Sound/symbol association; Writing words and letters

COMBINING CONSONANTS

Look at the picture in each box.
Look at the letters in each box.
Write the blend that you hear at the beginning of each pictured word.
Then color the pictures.

_____

ow

_____

are

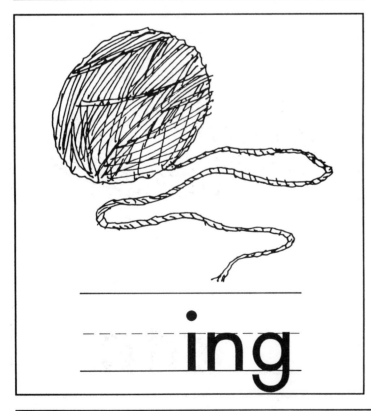

_____

ing

_____

og

Skills: Recognizing consonant blends; Sound/symbol association; Writing words and letters

COMBINING CONSONANTS

Look at the picture in each box.
Look at the letters in each box.
Write the blend that you hear at the beginning of each pictured word.
Then color the pictures.

ize

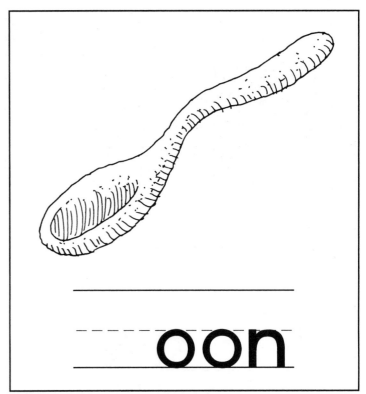

oon

ick

ate

Skills: Recognizing consonant blends; Sound/symbol association; Writing words and letters

COMBINING CONSONANTS

Look at the picture in each box.
Look at the letters in each box.
Write the blend that you hear at the beginning of each pictured word.
Then color the pictures.

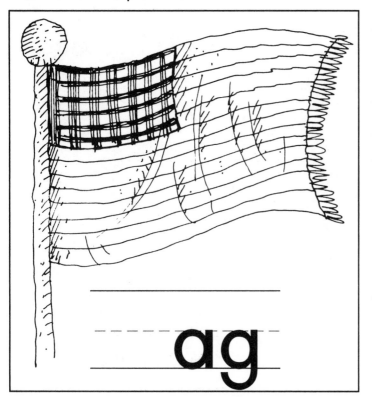

_ _ _ _ ag

_ _ _ _ ain

_ _ _ _ own

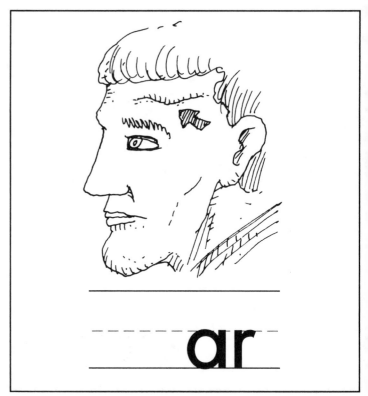

_ _ _ _ ar

Skills: Recognizing consonant blends; Sound/symbol association; Writing words and letters

COMBINING CONSONANTS

Look at the picture in each box.
Look at the letters in each box.
Write the blend that you hear at the beginning of each pictured word.
Then color the pictures.

_____

ape

_____

one

_____

ing

_____

ile

Skills: Recognizing consonant blends; Sound/symbol association; Writing words and letters

COMBINING CONSONANTS

Some consonant blends are at the end of a word.
Look at the picture in each box.
Look at the letters in each box.
Write the consonant blend -**lt** or -**ft** that is missing.
Then color the picture.

ra

qui

be

gi

Skills: Recognizing final consonant blends; Sound/symbol association; Writing words and letters

COMBINING CONSONANTS

Some consonant blends are at the end of a word.
Look at the picture in each box.
Look at the letters in each box.
Write the consonant blend **-ld** or **-nd** that is missing.
Then color the picture.

sa

chi

go

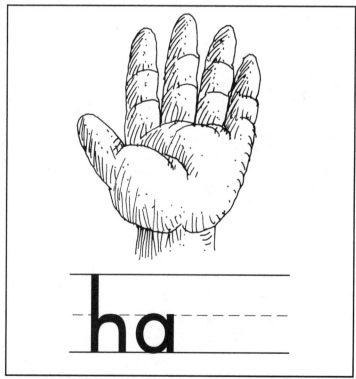

ha

Skills: Recognizing final consonant blends; Sound/symbol association; Writing words and letters

COMBINING CONSONANTS

Some consonant blends are at the end of a word.
Look at the picture in each box.
Look at the letters in each box.
Write the consonant blend **-mp** or **-nk** that is missing.
Then color the picture.

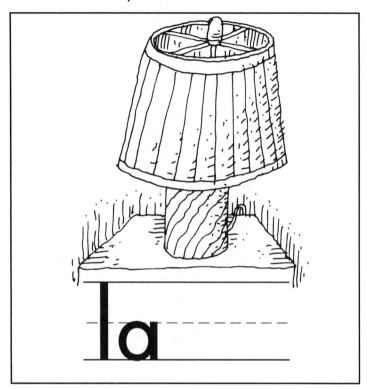

la

si

tru

sta

Skills: Recognizing final consonant blends; Sound/symbol association; Writing words and letters

COMBINING CONSONANTS

Some consonant blends are at the end of a word.
Look at the picture in each box.
Look at the letters in each box.
Write the consonant blend **-st** or **-nt** that is missing.
Then color the picture.

ne

pla

pai

che

Skills: Recognizing final consonant blends; Sound/symbol association; Writing words and letters

COMBINING CONSONANTS

Some consonant blends are at the end of a word.
Look at the picture in each box.
Look at the letters in each box.
Write the consonant blend -**sp** or -**sk** that is missing.
Then color the picture.

ma ____

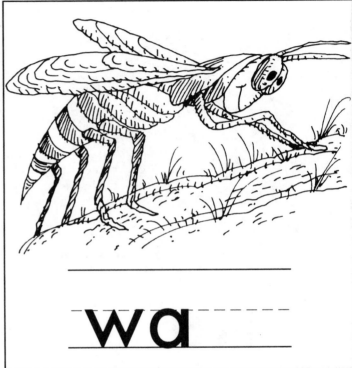

wa ____

cla ____

de ____

Skills: Recognizing final consonant blends; Sound/symbol association; Writing words and letters

COMBINING CONSONANTS

Some consonant blends are at the end of a word.
Look at the picture in each box.
Look at the letters in each box.
Write the consonant blend -**lk** or -**ng** that is missing.
Then color the picture.

mi

si

swi

ri

Skills: Recognizing final consonant blends; Sound/symbol association; Writing words and letters

COMBINING CONSONANTS

Look at the picture in each box.
Look at the words in each box.
Circle the word that names each picture.
Then color the pictures.

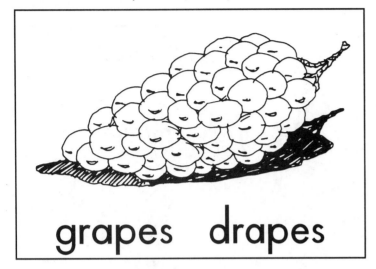

grapes   drapes

fly   frog

truck   brick

pray   plant

blanket   brown

crown   clown

Skills: Recognizing consonant blends; Sound/symbol association

COMBINING CONSONANTS

Look at the picture in each box.
Look at the words in each box.
Circle the word that names each picture.
Then color the pictures.

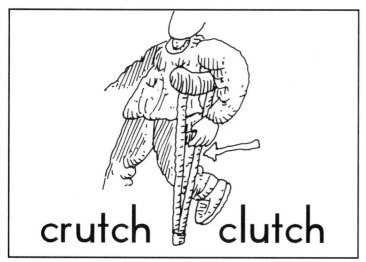

crutch   clutch

blink   bride

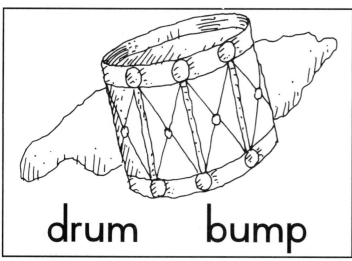

drum   bump

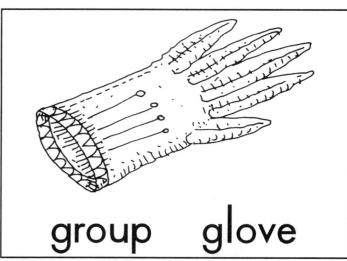

group   glove

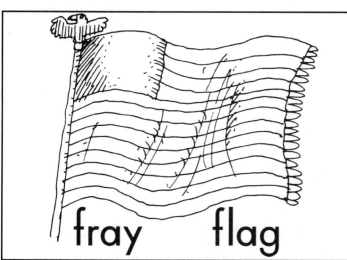

fray   flag

present   pleasant

Skills: Recognizing consonant blends; Sound/symbol association

COMBINING CONSONANTS

Look at the picture in each box.
Look at the words in each box.
Circle the word that names each picture.
Then color the pictures.

spade   slide

skunk   sleep

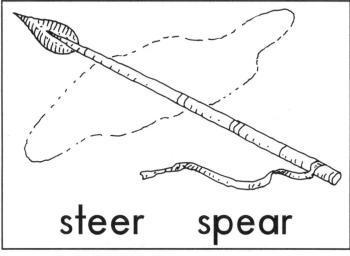

steer   spear

stamp   salad

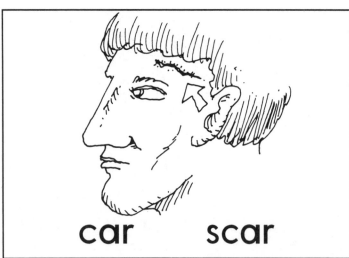

car   scar

swing   small

Skills: Recognizing consonant blends; Sound/symbol association

COMBINING CONSONANTS

Look at the picture in each box.
Look at the words in each box.
Circle the word that names each picture.
Then color the pictures.

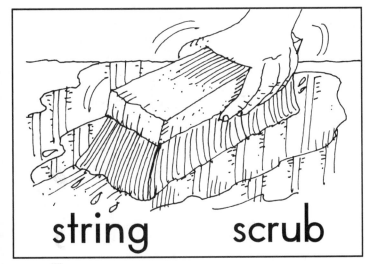

string   scrub

square   spurt

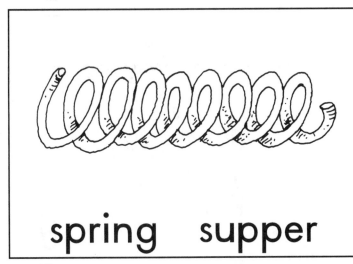

spring   supper

stop   street

sprinkler   stout

some   smoke

Skills: Recognizing consonant blends; Sound/symbol association

COMBINING CONSONANTS

Look at the picture in each box.
Look at the words in each box.
Circle the word that names each picture.
Then color the pictures.

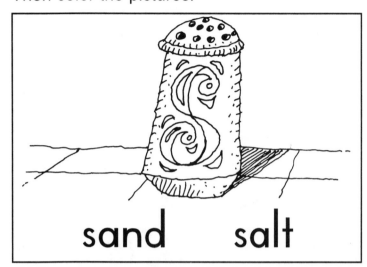

sand   salt

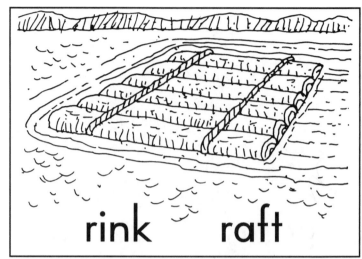

rink   raft

desk   dust

plank   plant

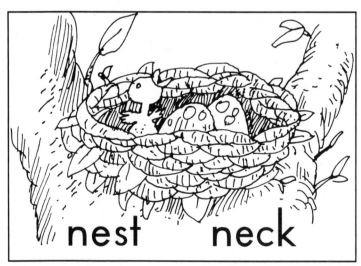

nest   neck

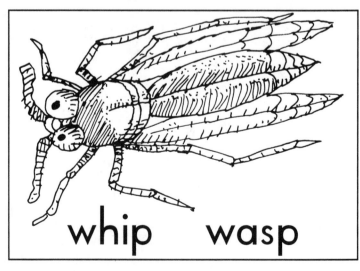

whip   wasp

Skills: Recognizing consonant blends; Sound/symbol association

COMBINING CONSONANTS

Sh is the sound you hear at the beginning of ship.
Look at the pictures on this page.
Draw a line from the **sh** to each picture whose name begins with the **sh** sound.

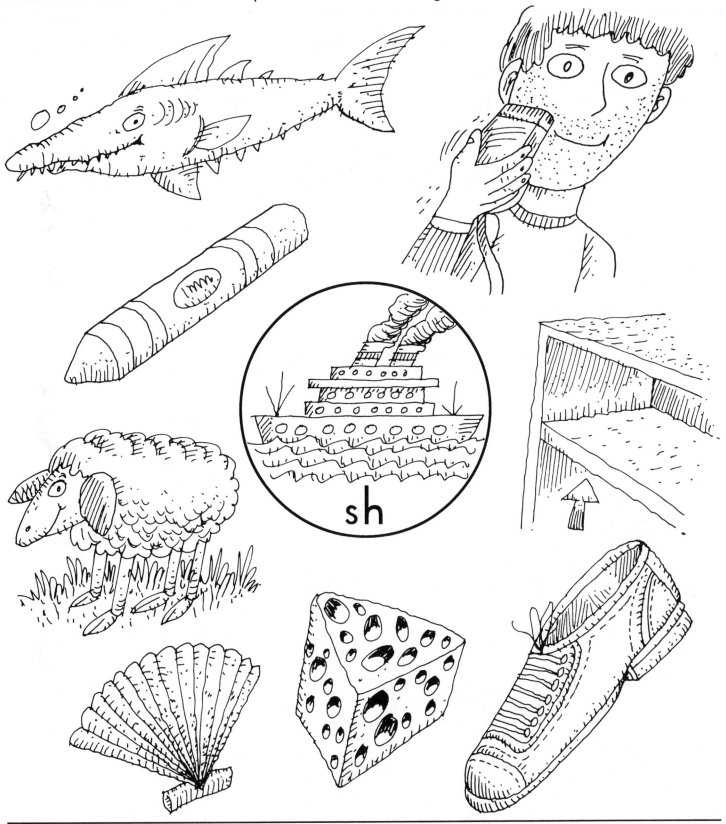

sh

Skills: Recognition of the consonant digraph "sh"; Sound/symbol association

COMBINING CONSONANTS

Ch is the sound you hear at the beginning of cheese.
Look at the pictures on this page.
Draw a line from the **ch** to each picture whose name begins with the **ch** sound.

ch

COMBINING CONSONANTS

Wh is the sound you hear at the beginning of whale.
Look at the pictures on this page.
Draw a line from the **wh** to each picture whose name begins with the **wh** sound.

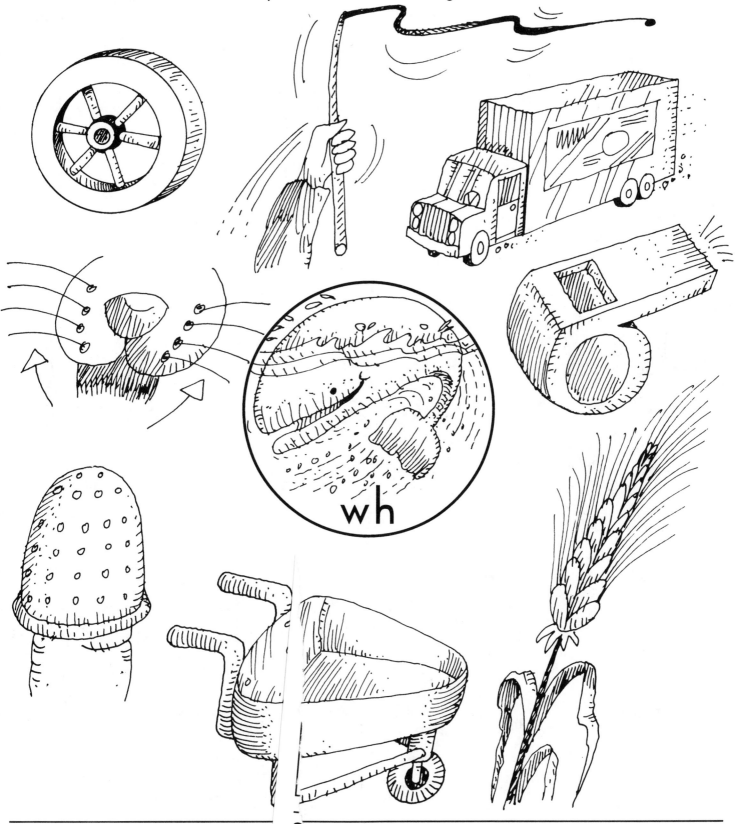

COMBINING CONSONANTS

Th is the sound you hear at the beginning of thorn.
Look at the pictures on this page.
Draw a line from the **th** to each picture whose name begins with the **th** sound.

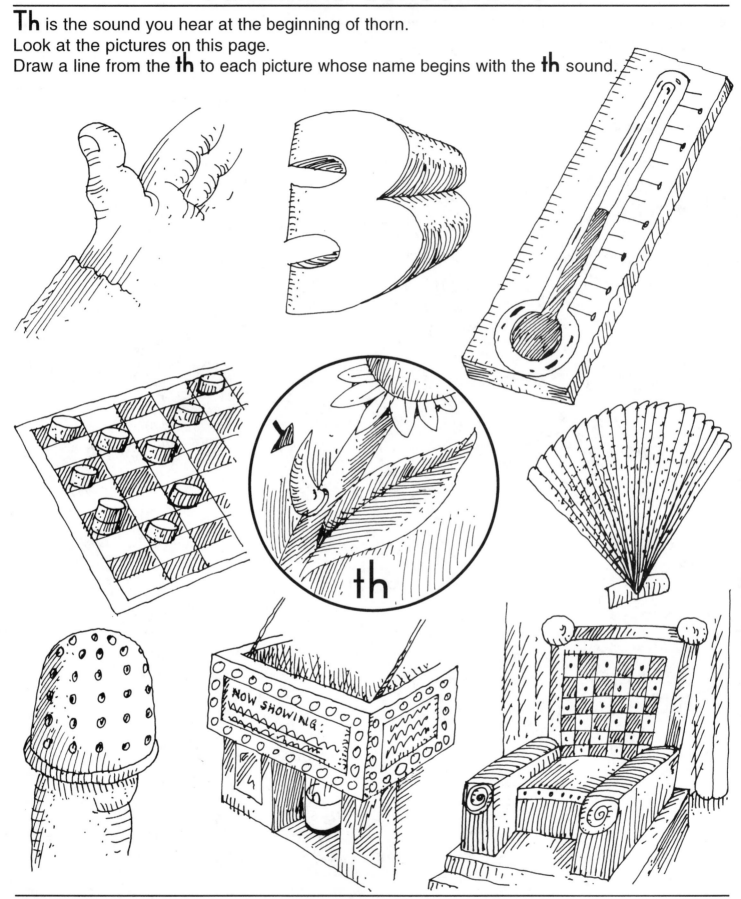

Skills: Recognition of the consonant digraph "th"; Sound/symbol association

COMBINING CONSONANTS

Look at the picture in each shell.

Say the name of each picture and listen to the beginning of the word.

If you hear the **th** sound, color the picture green.

If you hear the **wh** sound, color the picture blue.

If you hear the **ch** sound, color the picture red.

If you hear the **sh** sound, color the picture yellow.

Skills: Recognition of consonant digraphs; Sound/symbol association; Following complex directions

COMBINING CONSONANTS

Look at the picture in each cherry.
Say the name of each picture and listen to the beginning of the word.
If you hear the **th** sound, color the picture green.
If you hear the **wh** sound, color the picture blue.
If you hear the **ch** sound, color the picture red.
If you hear the **sh** sound, color the picture yellow.

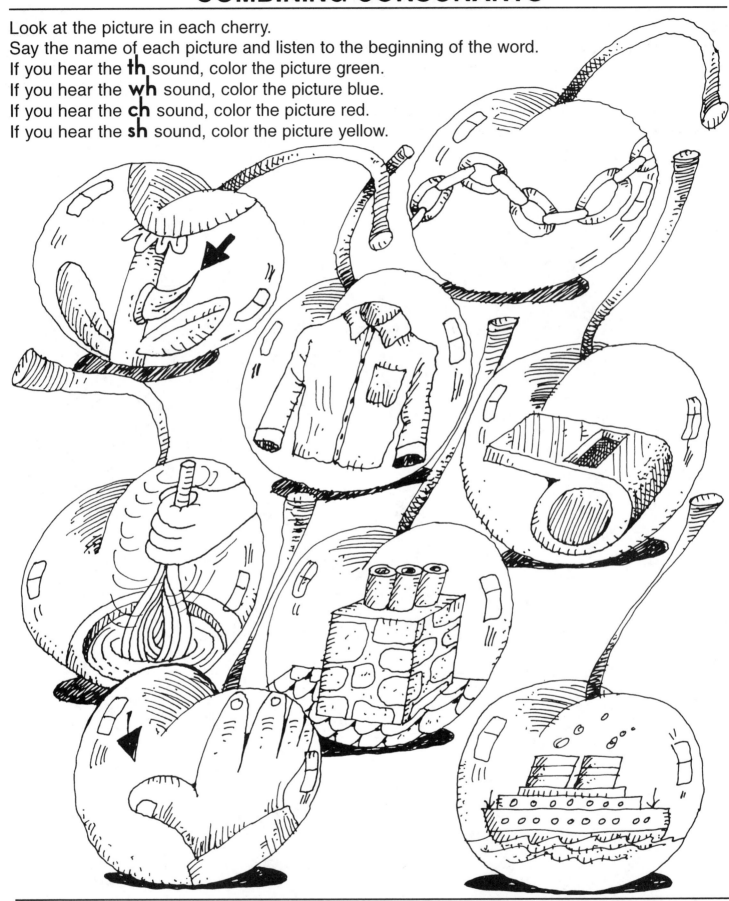

Skills: Recognition of consonant digraphs; Sound/symbol association; Following complex directions

226

COMBINING CONSONANTS

Look at the picture in each whale.
Say the name of each picture and listen to the beginning of the word.
If you hear the **th** sound, color the picture green.
If you hear the **wh** sound, color the picture blue.
If you hear the **ch** sound, color the picture red.
If you hear the **sh** sound, color the picture yellow.

Skills: Recognition of consonant digraphs; Sound/symbol association; Following complex directions

227

COMBINING CONSONANTS

Look at the words in the box.
Then look at each picture near the puzzle.
Write the word that names each picture in the puzzle.

| shelf | chief | thimble | wheel |

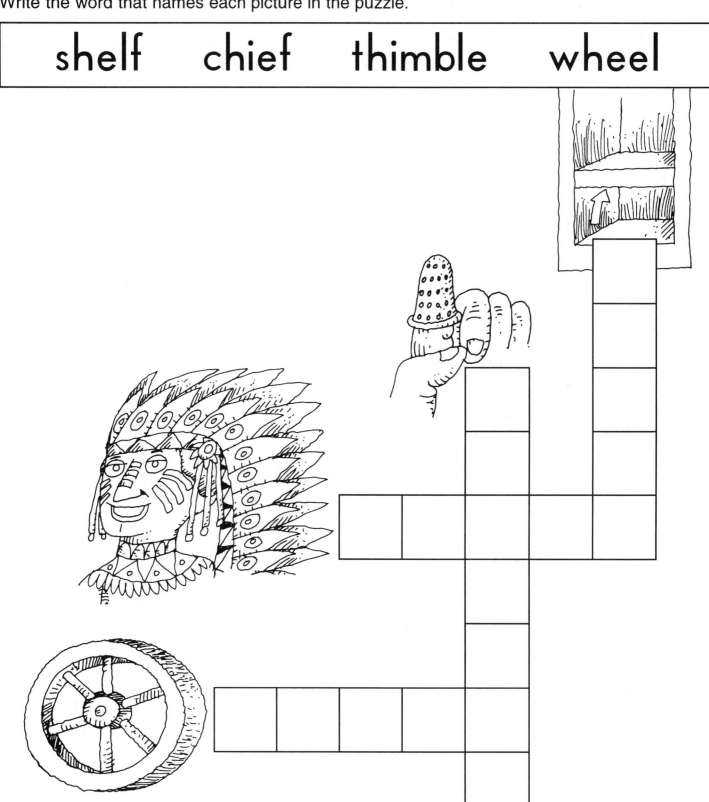

Skills: Recognition of consonant digraphs; Writing words; Following complex directions

COMBINING CONSONANTS

Look at the words in the box.
Then look at each picture near the puzzle.
Write the word that names each picture in the puzzle.

cherry   whistle   thumb   shell

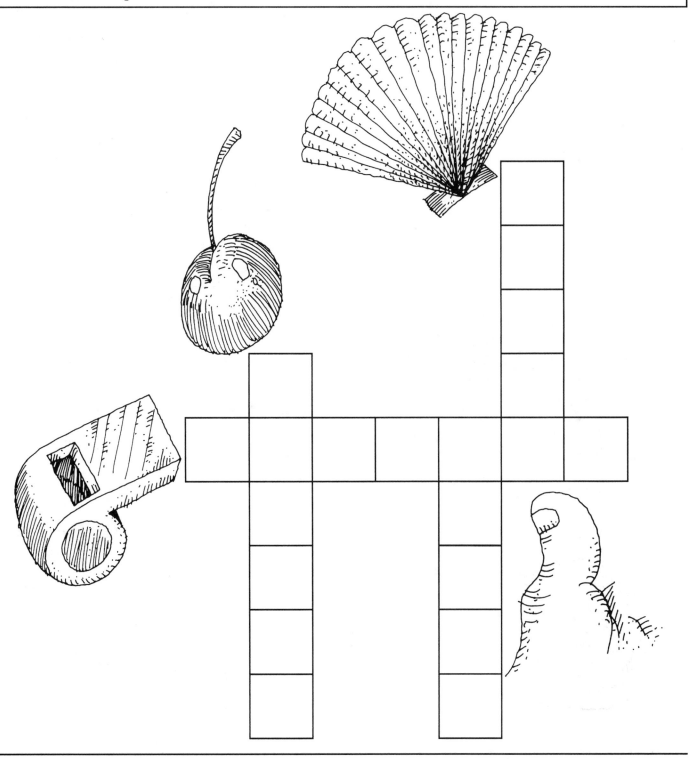

Skills: Recognition of consonant digraphs; Writing words; Following complex directions

COMBINING CONSONANTS

Look at the picture in each box.
Look at the letters under each picture.
Say the name of each picture and listen to the ending sound.
Circle the letters that make the sound you hear at the end of each word.

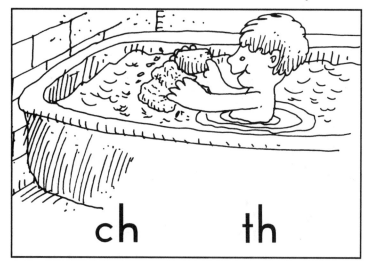

ch   th

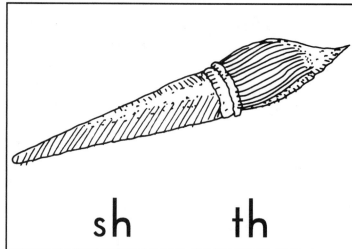

sh   th

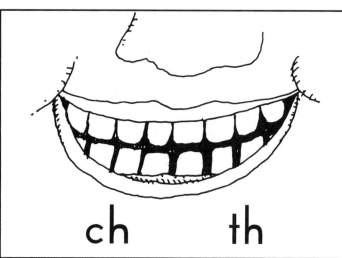

ch   th

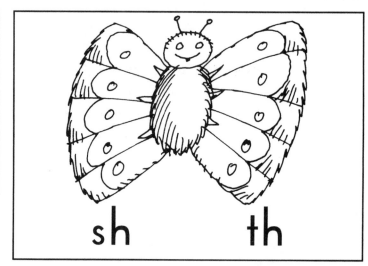

sh   th

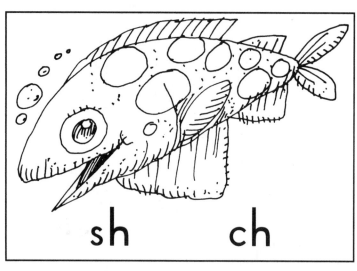

sh   ch

th   ch

Skills: Recognition of final consonant digraphs; Sound/symbol association; Auditory discrimination

COMBINING CONSONANTS

Look at the picture in each box.
Look at the letters under each picture.
Say the name of each picture and listen to the ending sound.
Circle the letters that make the sound you hear at the end of each word.

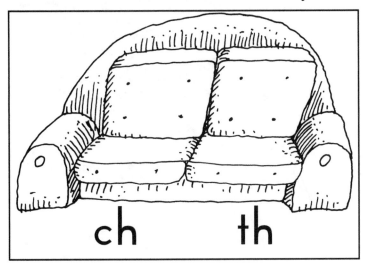

ch   th

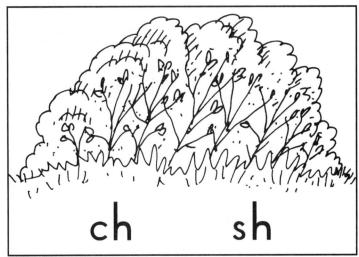

ch   sh

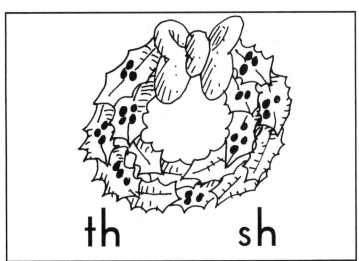

th   sh

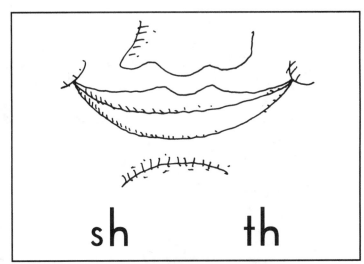

sh   th

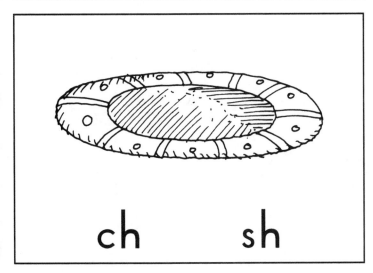

ch   sh

ch   sh

Skills: Recognition of final consonant digraphs; Sound/symbol association; Auditory discrimination

COMBINING CONSONANTS

Ck is the sound you hear at the end of lock.
Look at the pictures on this page.
Draw a line from the **ck** to each picture whose name ends with the **ck** sound.

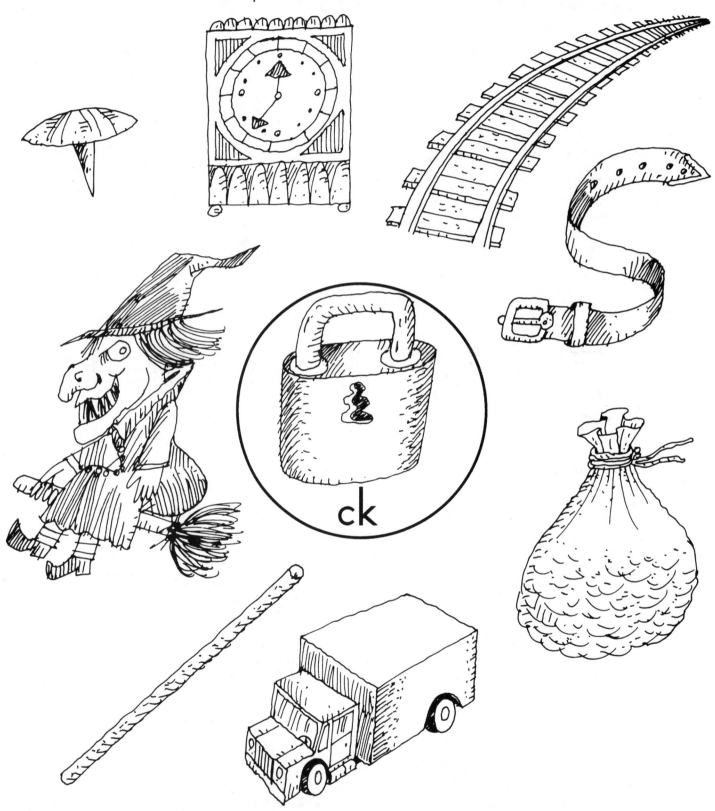

Skills: Recognition of the final consonant digraph "ck"; Sound/symbol association

COMBINING CONSONANTS

Tch is the sound you hear at the end of catch.
Look at the pictures on this page.
Draw a line from the **tch** to each picture whose name ends with the **tch** sound.

tch

Skills: Recognition of the final consonant digraph "tch"; Sound/symbol association

COMBINING CONSONANTS

Look at the picture in each box.
Look at the letters under each picture.
Say the name of each picture and listen to the ending sound.
Circle the letters that make the sound you hear at the end of each word.

tch   ck

ck   tch

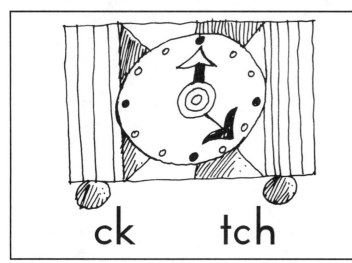

ck   tch

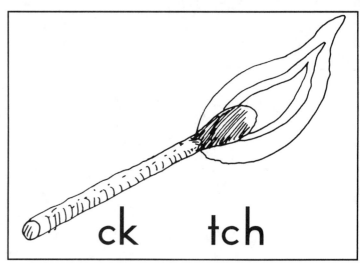

ck   tch

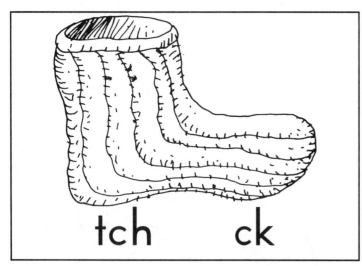

tch   ck

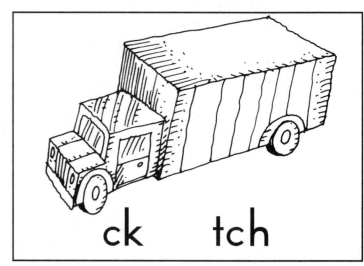

ck   tch

Skills: Recognition of final consonant digraphs; Sound/symbol association; Auditory discrimination

COMBINING CONSONANTS

Look at the consonant digraphs in the box at the top of the page.
Say the name of the picture in each box.
Listen carefully to the beginning and ending sounds.
Look at the letters in each box.
Write the letters that stand for the consonant digraph you hear.

sh   th   ch   wh   ck   tch

_____ ell

du _____

_____ air

_____ iskers

cru _____

umb _____

Skills: Recognition of beginning and final consonant digraphs; Sound/symbol association;
Auditory discrimination; Writing letters

235

COMBINING CONSONANTS

Look at the consonant digraphs in the box at the top of the page.
Say the name of the picture in each box.
Listen carefully to the beginning and ending sounds.
Look at the letters in each box.
Write the letters that stand for the consonant digraph you hear.

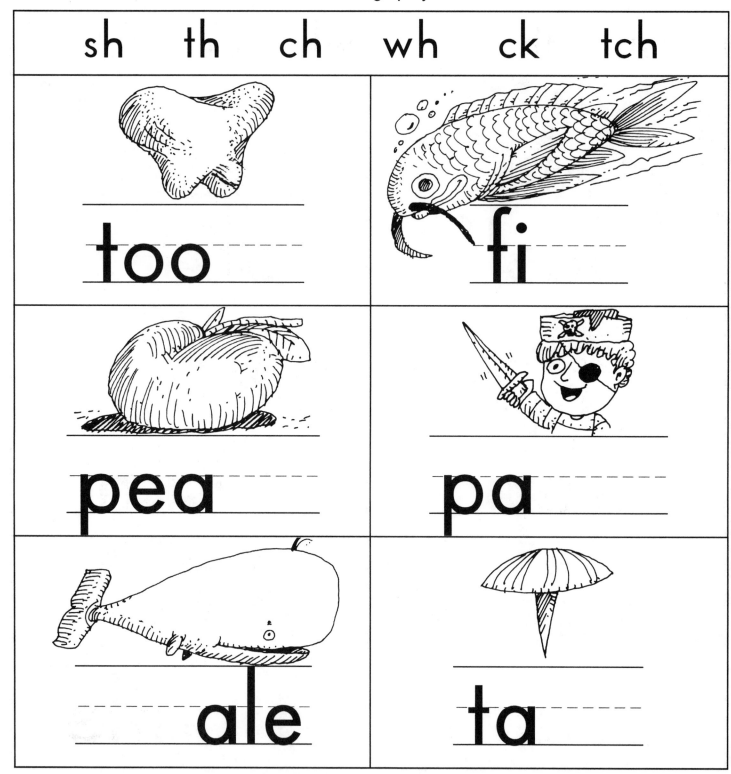

| sh | th | ch | wh | ck | tch |

too ___

fi ___

pea ___

pa ___

ale ___

ta ___

Skills: Recognition of beginning and final consonant digraphs; Sound/symbol association;
Auditory discrimination; Writing letters

COMBINING CONSONANTS

Look at the consonant digraphs in the box at the top of the page.
Say the name of the picture in each box.
Listen carefully to the beginning and ending sounds.
Look at the letters in each box.
Write the letters that stand for the consonant digraph you hear.

sh   th   ch   wh   ck   tch

ba

sti

wa

orn

ain

istle

Skills: Recognition of beginning and final consonant digraphs; Sound/symbol association;
Auditory discrimination; Writing letters

COMBINING CONSONANTS

Look at the consonant digraphs in the box at the top of the page.
Say the name of the picture in each box.
Listen carefully to the beginning and ending sounds.
Look at the letters in each box.
Write the letters that stand for the consonant digraph you hear.

sh   th   ch   wh   ck   tch

_____ oe

_____ in

bru _____

_____ ip

_____ eese

_____ irt

Skills: Recognition of beginning and final consonant digraphs; Sound/symbol association;
Auditory discrimination; Writing letters

238

COMBINING CONSONANTS

Look at the pictures on the left.
Look at the pictures on the right.
Draw lines between the pictures that end with the same sound.
Then color the pictures.

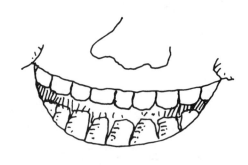

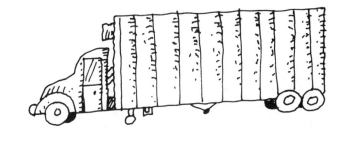

Skills: Recognition of consonant digraphs; Sound/symbol association; Auditory discrimination

COMBINING CONSONANTS

Look at the pictures on the left.
Look at the pictures on the right.
Draw lines between the pictures that begin with the same sound.
Then color the pictures.

Skills: Recognition of consonant digraphs; Sound/symbol association; Auditory discrimination

WORD FAMILIES

Look at the picture in the center circle.
Listen to the **at** sound you hear at the end of cat.
Look at the rest of the pictures on this page.
Circle the pictures that contain the sound of **at**.

Skills: Identification of the "at" word family; Association between sounds, symbols, and words; Recognizing rhyming words

WORD FAMILIES

Hat is in the **at** family.
There are many other words in the **at** family.
Look at the letters in the box below.
Use the letters to make words in the **at** family.
Can you think of more words in the **at** family?

 hat

m	r	c	b

Skills: Identification of the "at" word family; Association between sounds, symbols, and words; Forming new words

WORD FAMILIES

Look at the picture in the center circle.
Listen to the **an** sound you hear at the end of can.
Look at the rest of the pictures on this page.
Circle the pictures that contain the sound of **an**.

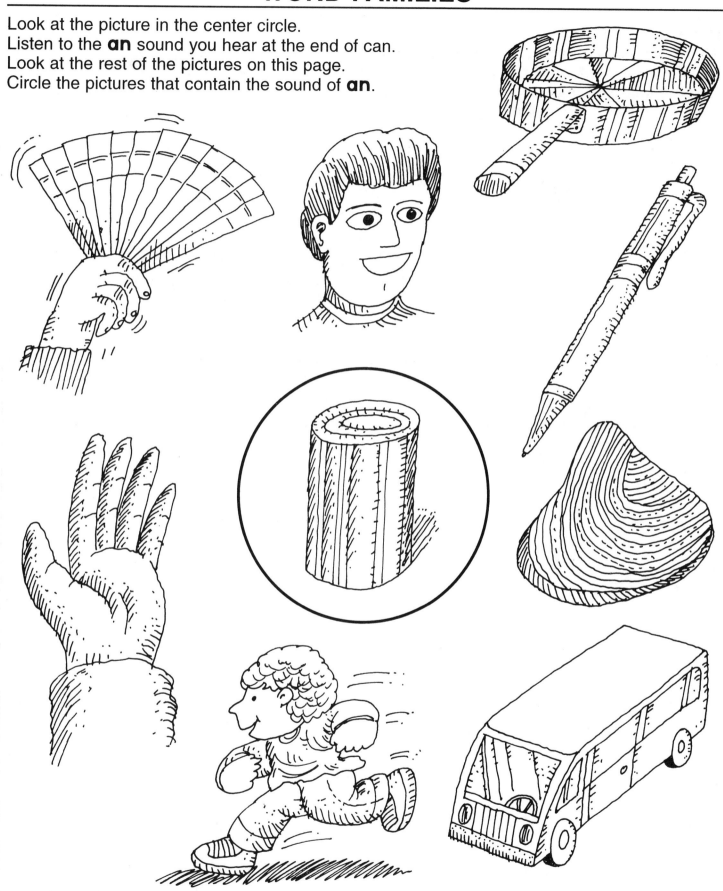

Skills: Identification of the "an" word family; Association between sounds, symbols, and words; Recognizing rhyming words

WORD FAMILIES

Fan is in the **an** family.
There are many other words in the **an** family.
Look at the letters in the box below.
Use the letters to make words in the **an** family.
Can you think of more words in the **an** family?

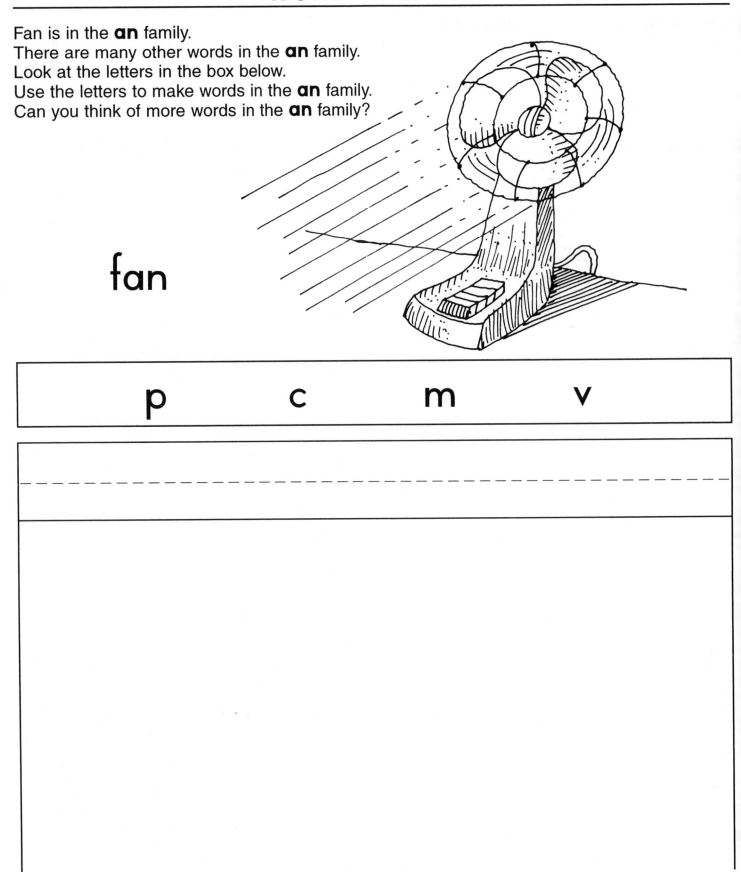

fan

p	c	m	v

Skills: Identification of the "an" word family; Association between sounds, symbols, and words; Forming new words

244

WORD FAMILIES

Look at the picture in the center circle.
Listen to the **et** sound you hear at the end of pet.
Look at the rest of the pictures on this page.
Circle the pictures that contain the sound of **et**.

Skills: Identification of the "et" word family; Association between sounds, symbols, and words; Recognizing rhyming words

WORD FAMILIES

Jet is in the **et** family.
There are many other words in the **et** family.
Look at the letters in the box below.
Use the letters to make words in the **et** family.
Can you think of more words in the **et** family?

jet

| n | p | w | m |

Skills: Identification of the "et" word family; Association between sounds, symbols, and words; Forming new words

WORD FAMILIES

Look at the picture in the center circle.
Listen to the **en** sound you hear at the end of pen.
Look at the rest of the pictures on this page.
Circle the pictures that contain the sound of **en**.

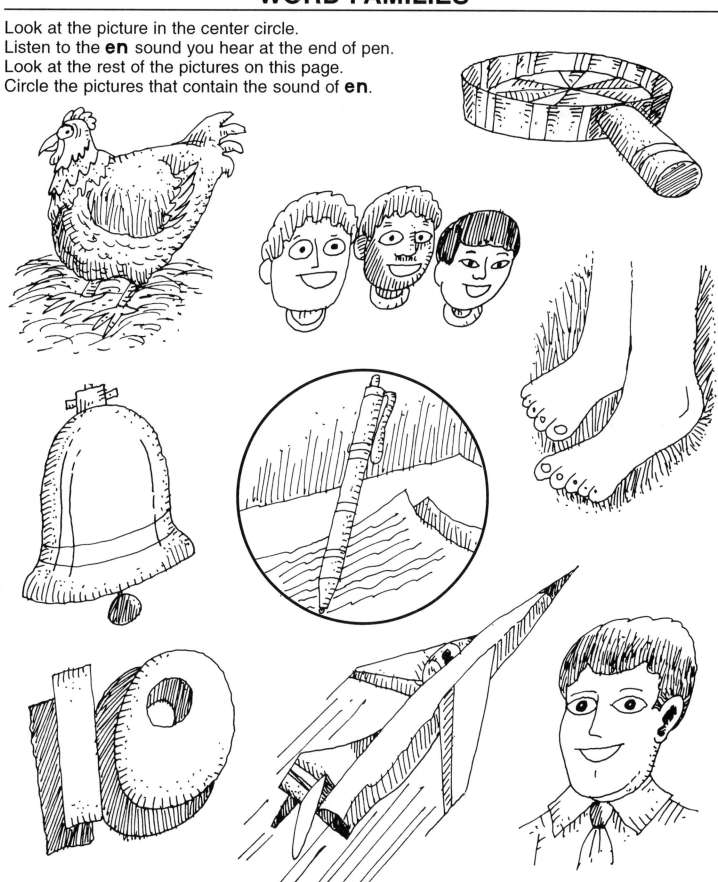

Skills: Identification of the "en" word family; Association between sounds, symbols, and words; Recognizing rhyming words

WORD FAMILIES

Hen is in the **en** family.
There are many other words in the **en** family.
Look at the letters in the box below.
Use the letters to make words in the **en** family.
Can you think of more words in the **en** family?

hen

m	d	p	t

Skills: Identification of the "en" word family; Association between sounds, symbols, and words; Forming new words

WORD FAMILIES

Look at the picture in the center circle.
Listen to the **in** sound you hear at the end of pin.
Look at the rest of the pictures on this page.
Circle the pictures that contain the sound of **in**.

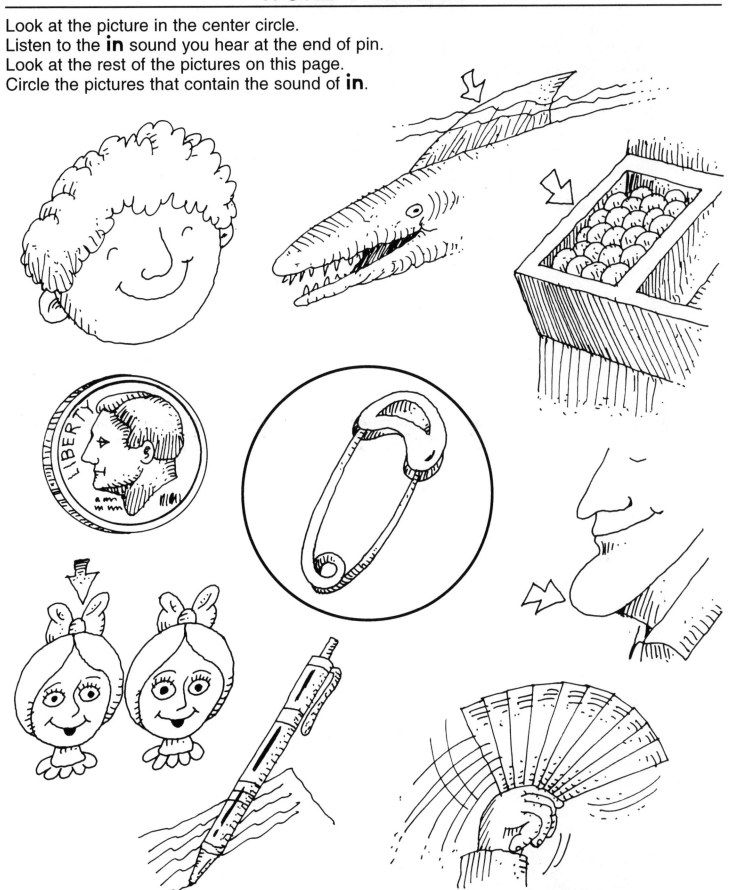

Skills: Identification of the "in" word family; Association between sounds, symbols, and words; Recognizing rhyming words

WORD FAMILIES

Pin is in the **in** family.
There are many other words in the **in** family.
Look at the letters in the box below.
Use the letters to make words in the **in** family.
Can you think of more words in the **in** family?

pin

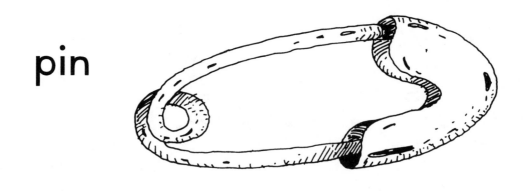

f	t	w	th

Skills: Identification of the "in" word family; Association between sounds, symbols, and words; Forming new words

WORD FAMILIES

Look at the picture in the center circle.
Listen to the **ip** sound you hear at the end of ship.
Look at the rest of the pictures on this page.
Circle the pictures that contain the sound of **ip**.

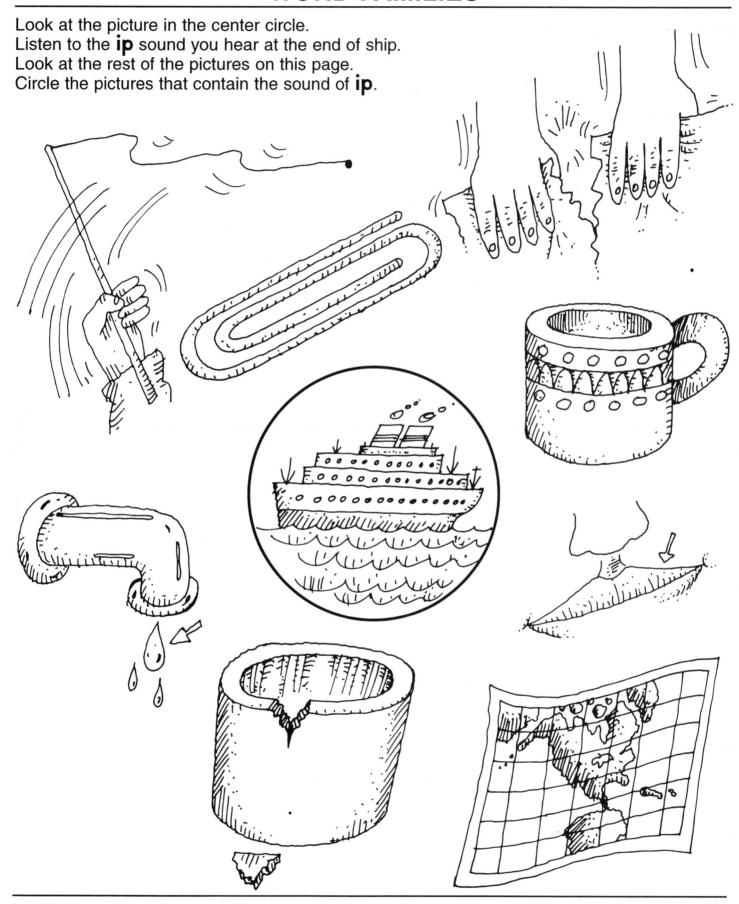

Skills: Identification of the "ip" word family; Association between sounds, symbols, and words; Recognizing rhyming words

WORD FAMILIES

Clip is in the **ip** family.
There are many other words in the **ip** family.
Look at the letters in the box below.
Use the letters to make words in the **ip** family.
Can you think of more words in the **ip** family?

clip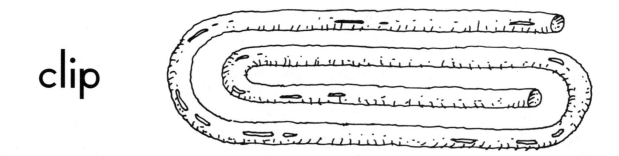

s	t	l	r

Skills: Identification of the "ip" word family; Association between sounds, symbols, and words; Forming new words

WORD FAMILIES

Look at the picture in the center circle.
Listen to the **og** sound you hear at the end of jog.
Look at the rest of the pictures on this page.
Circle the pictures that contain the sound of **og**.

Skills: Identification of the "og" word family; Association between sounds, symbols, and words; Recognizing rhyming words

WORD FAMILIES

Frog is in the **og** family.
There are many other words in the **og** family.
Look at the letters in the box below.
Use the letters to make words in the **og** family.
Can you think of more words in the **og** family?

frog

h   l   j   f

Skills: Identification of the "og" word family; Association between sounds, symbols, and words; Forming new words

WORD FAMILIES

Look at the picture in the center circle.
Listen to the **ock** sound you hear at the end of clock.
Look at the rest of the pictures on this page.
Circle the pictures that contain the sound of **ock**.

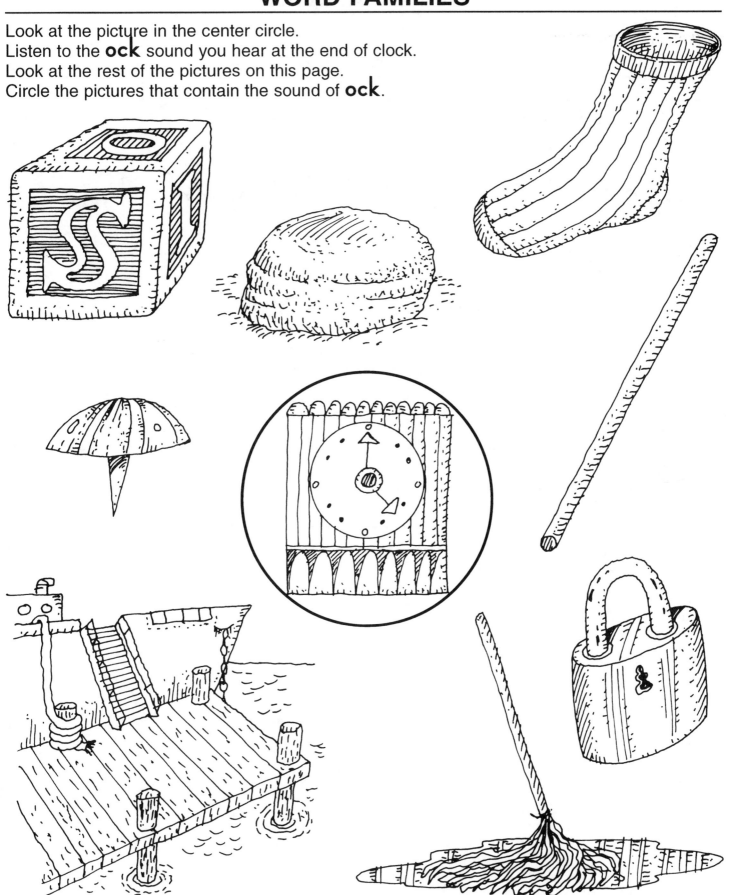

Skills: Identification of the "ock" word family; Association between sounds, symbols, and words; Recognizing rhyming words

WORD FAMILIES

Lock is in the **ock** family.
There are many other words in the **ock** family.
Look at the letters in the box below.
Use the letters to make words in the **ock** family.
Can you think of more words in the **ock** family?

lock

cl   r   d   s

Skills: Identification of the "ock" word family; Association between sounds, symbols, and words; Forming new words

WORD FAMILIES

Look at the picture in the center circle.
Listen to the **ub** sound you hear at the end of cub.
Look at the rest of the pictures on this page.
Circle the pictures that contain the sound of **ub**.

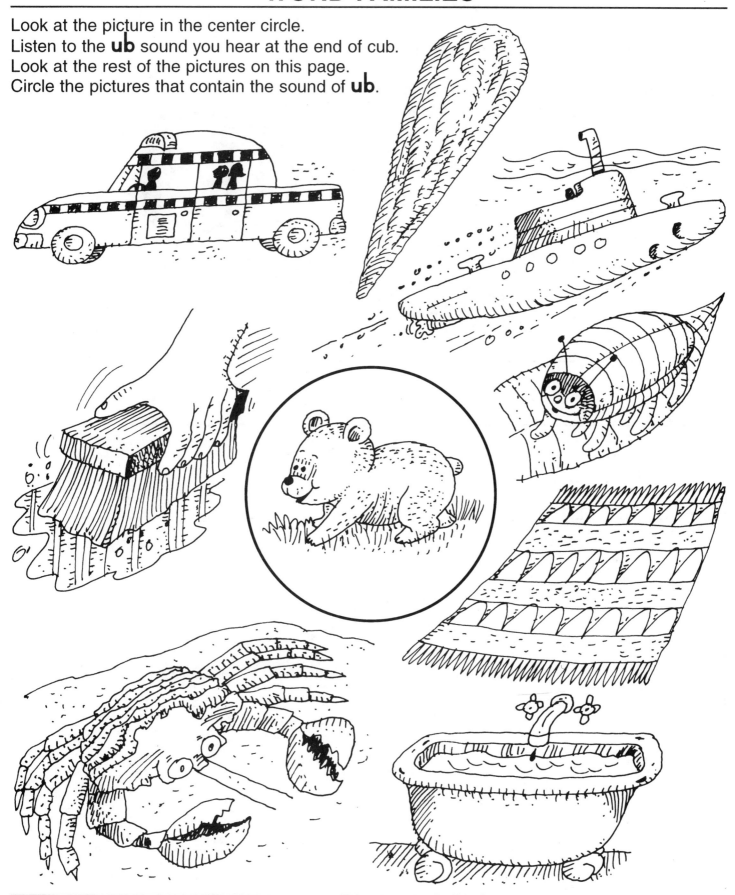

Skills: Identification of the "ub" word family; Association between sounds, symbols, and words; Recognizing rhyming words

WORD FAMILIES

Club is in the **ub** family.
There are many other words in the **ub** family.
Look at the letters in the box below.
Use the letters to make words in the **ub** family.
Can you think of more words in the **ub** family?

club

t	s	r	h	

Skills: Identification of the "ub" word family; Association between sounds, symbols, and words; Forming new words

WORD FAMILIES

Look at the picture in the center circle.
Listen to the **ug** sound you hear at the end of bug.
Look at the rest of the pictures on this page.
Circle the pictures that contain the sound of **ug**.

Skills: Identification of the "ug" word family; Association between sounds, symbols, and words; Recognizing rhyming words

WORD FAMILIES

Mug is in the **ug** family.
There are many other words in the **ug** family.
Look at the letters in the box below.
Use the letters to make words in the **ug** family.
Can you think of more words in the **ug** family?

mug

b   r   j   t

Skills: Identification of the "ug" word family; Association between sounds, symbols, and words; Forming new words

SYNONYMS

Synonyms are words that have the same or almost the same meanings.
Look at the word in each magic lamp.
Look at the words in the box at the top of the page.
In each magic carpet, write a word from the box that is a synonym to the word in the lamp.

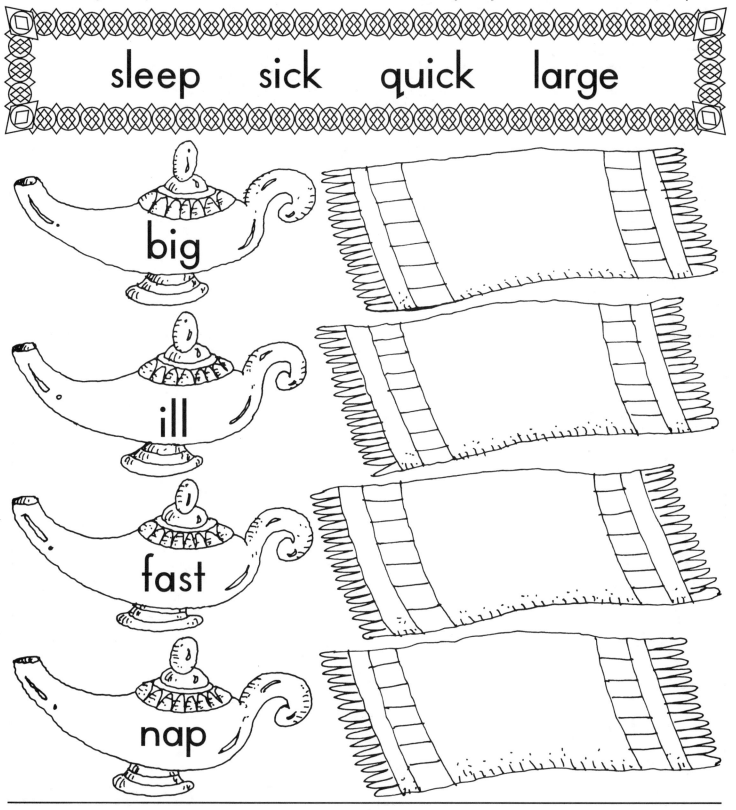

sleep   sick   quick   large

big

ill

fast

nap

Skills: Identifying synonyms; Vocabulary development

261

SYNONYMS

Synonyms are words that have the same or almost the same meanings.
Look at the word in each baseball.
Look at the words in the box at the top of the page.
In each bat, write a word from the box that is a synonym to the word in the ball.

glad   small   shut   glove

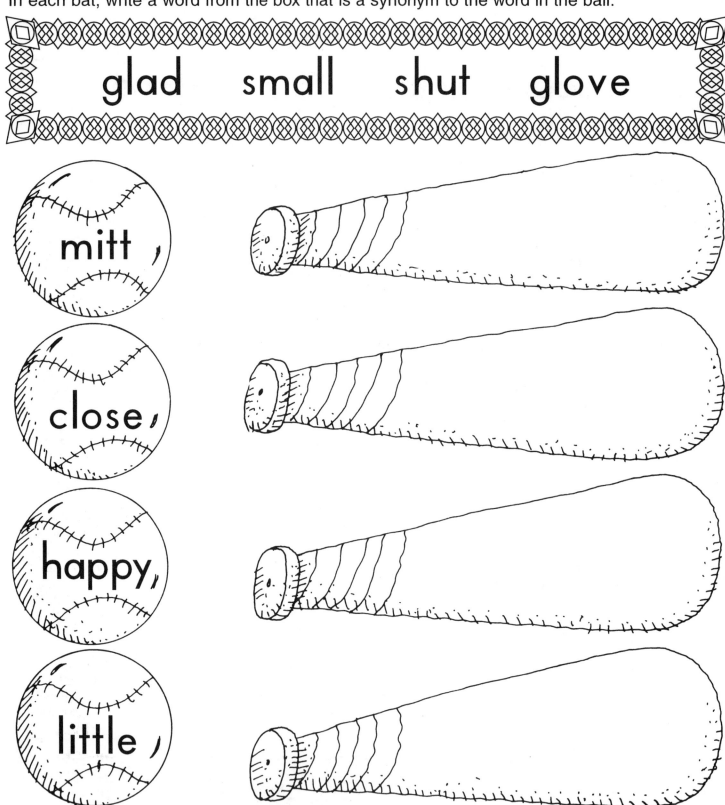

SYNONYMS

Synonyms are words that have the same or almost the same meanings.
Look at the word in each bird.
Look at the words in the box at the top of the page.
In each nest, write a word from the box that is a synonym to the word in the bird.

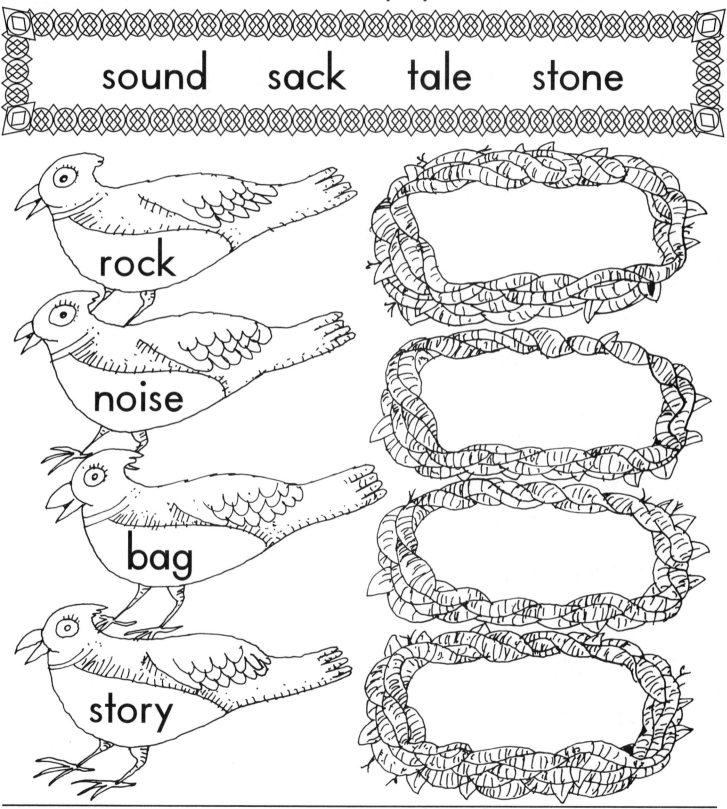

sound   sack   tale   stone

rock

noise

bag

story

Skills: Identifying synonyms; Vocabulary development

SYNONYMS

Synonyms are words that have the same or almost the same meanings.
Look at the word in each fish.
Look at the words in the box at the top of the page.
In each fishbowl, write a word from the box that is a synonym to the word in the fish.

kind   simple   friend   present

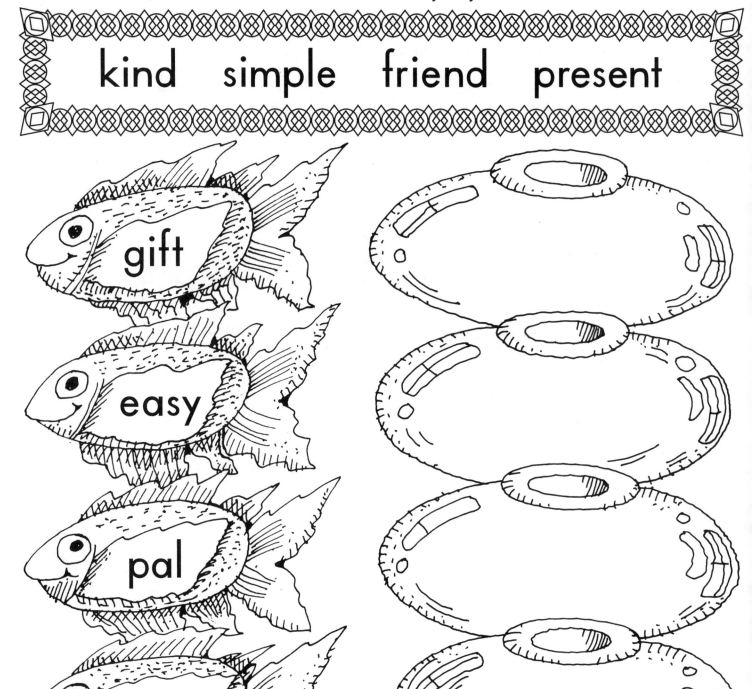

Skills: Identifying synonyms; Vocabulary development

SYNONYMS

Synonyms are words that have the same or almost the same meanings.
Look at the word in each mailbox.
Look at the words in the box at the top of the page.
In each letter, write a word from the box that is a synonym to the word in the mailbox.

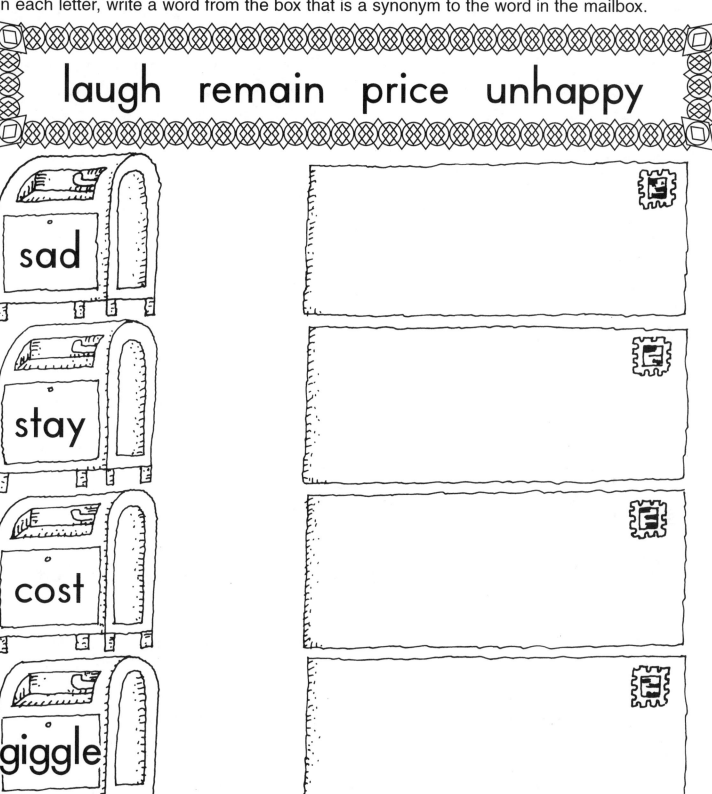

laugh   remain   price   unhappy

sad

stay

cost

giggle

Skills: Identifying synonyms; Vocabulary development

265

SYNONYMS

Synonyms are words that have the same or almost the same meanings.
Read each sentence and look at the underlined word.
Then read the words in the box under the sentence.
Circle the word that is a synonym to the underlined word.

My <u>pal</u> and I went to the park.

funny	friend	dog

We brought our <u>pretty</u> kite.

beautiful	happy	broken

We were <u>sad</u> that the kite got stuck.

nice	little	unhappy

A <u>kind</u> man helped us.

tired	nice	noisy

Skills: Identifying synonyms; Vocabulary deveploment; Recognizing synonyms in a group of words

SYNONYMS

Synonyms are words that have the same or almost the same meanings.
Read each sentence and look at the underlined word.
Then read the words in the box under the sentence.
Circle the word that is a synonym to the underlined word.

Our <u>gang</u> went to the zoo today.

| friend | father | group |

The birds were really <u>loud</u>!

| beautiful | noisy | silly |

The lions <u>scared</u> us.

| frightened | laughed | joked |

The elephants were really <u>big</u>.

| ill | glad | huge |

Skills: Identifying synonyms; Vocabulary development; Recognizing synonyms in a group of words

SYNONYMS

Synonyms are words that have the same or almost the same meanings.
Read each sentence and look at the underlined word.
Then read the words in the box under the sentence.
Circle the word that is a synonym to the underlined word.

The ground was <u>moist</u> from the rain.

| colorful | wet | cold |

It was <u>hard</u> to run on the field.

| fun | silly | difficult |

We <u>picked</u> players for our game.

| chose | cleaned | slept |

We played soccer very <u>quickly</u>.

| slowly | fast | happily |

Skills: Identifying synonyms; Vocabulary development; Recognizing synonyms in a group of words

SYNONYMS

Synonyms are words that have the same or almost the same meanings.
Read each sentence and look at the underlined word.
Then read the words in the box under the sentence.
Circle the word that is a synonym to the underlined word.

It was a <u>chilly</u> and snowy day.

| hot | cold | rainy |

We filled <u>buckets</u> with snow.

| dolls | bricks | pails |

We made <u>heaps</u> of snow.

| jumps | cans | piles |

We made a <u>chubby</u> snowman.

| fat | bright | poor |

Skills: Identifying synonyms; Vocabulary development; Recognizing synonyms in a group of words

SYNONYMS

Synonyms are words that have the same or almost the same meanings.
Read each sentence and look at the underlined word.
Then read the words in the box under the sentence.
Circle the word that is a synonym to the underlined word.

Look at the little <u>bug</u>.

person	car	insect

It can <u>jump</u> so far!

leap	run	swim

We <u>caught</u> the bug in a jar.

hat	trapped	envelope

Someone forgot to <u>close</u> the jar.

shut	open	happy

Skills: Identifying synonyms; Vocabulary development; Recognizing synonyms in a group of words

SYNONYMS

Synonyms are words that have the same or almost the same meanings.
Look at the words in each beach ball.
Color the sections with words that are synonyms.

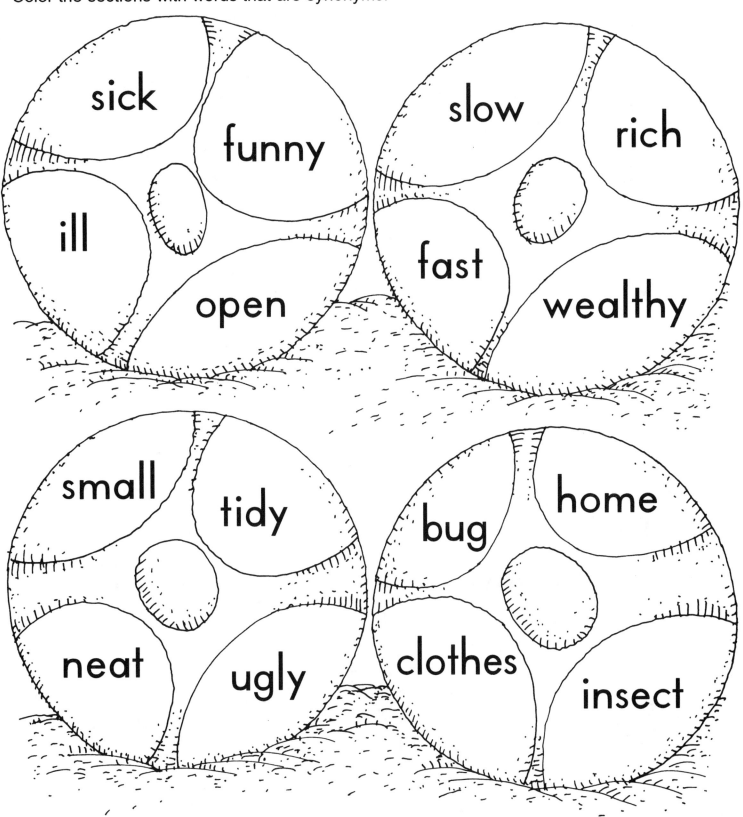

sick
funny
ill
open

slow
rich
fast
wealthy

small
tidy
neat
ugly

bug
home
clothes
insect

SYNONYMS

Synonyms are words that have the same or almost the same meanings.
Look at the words in each kite.
Color the sections with words that are synonyms.

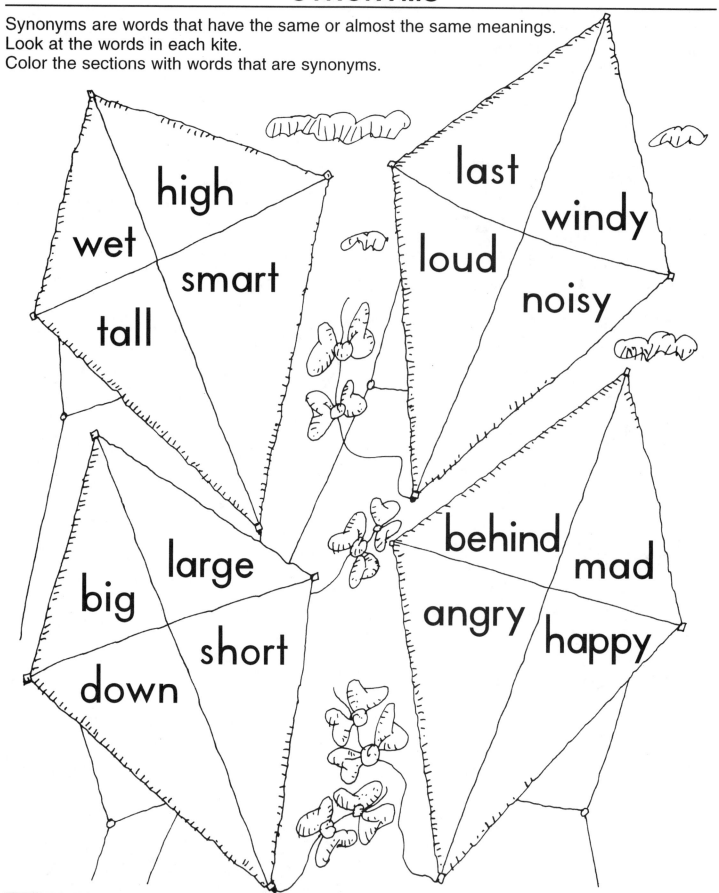

SYNONYMS

Synonyms are words that have the same or almost the same meanings.
Look at the words in each flag.
Color the sections with words that are synonyms.

car

sandwich

couch

sofa

sing

cry

weep

laugh

scare

jump

chilly

pants

shirt

trousers

hat

frighten

Skills: Identifying synonyms; Vocabulary development; Recognizing synonyms in a group of words

SYNONYMS

Synonyms are words that have the same or almost the same meanings.
Look at the words in each rainbow.
Color the sections with words that are synonyms.

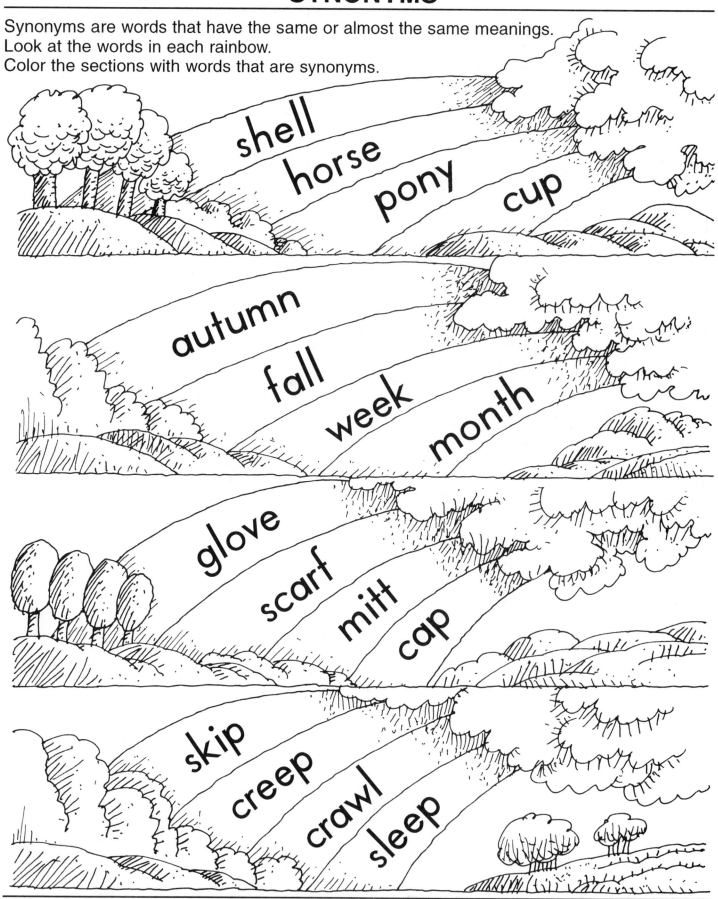

Skills: Identifying synonyms; Vocabulary development; Recognizing synonyms in a group of words

SYNONYMS

Synonyms are words that have the same or almost the same meanings.
Look at the words in each gift box.
Color the sections with words that are synonyms.

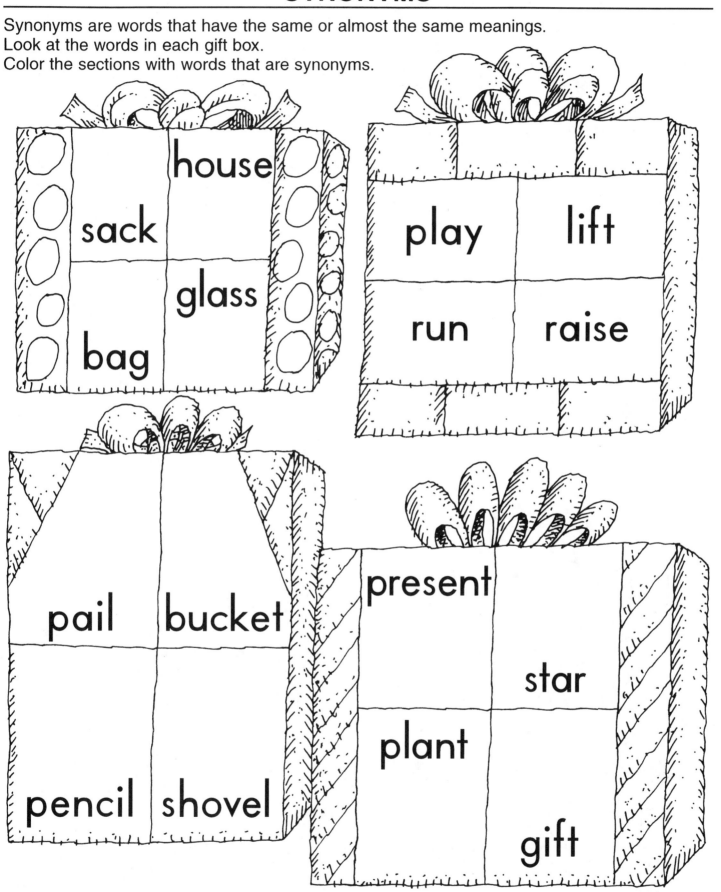

sack	house
	glass
bag	

play	lift
run	raise

pail	bucket
pencil	shovel

present	
	star
plant	
	gift

Skills: Identifying synonyms; Vocabulary development; Recognizing synonyms in a group of words

ANTONYMS

Antonyms are words that are opposites.
Look at the pictures and words on the left.
Look at the words and pictures on the right.
Draw lines to match the pairs of antonyms.
Then color the pictures.

front

hot

dry

clean

dirty

wet

cold

back

Skills: Recognizing antonyms; Vocabulary development

ANTONYMS

Antonyms are words that are opposites.
Look at the pictures and words on the left.
Look at the words and pictures on the right.
Draw lines to match the pairs of antonyms.
Then color the pictures.

asleep

sad

soft

full

happy

hard

empty

awake

Skills: Recognizing antonyms; Vocabulary development

ANTONYMS

Antonyms are words that are opposites.
Look at the pictures and words on the left.
Look at the words and pictures on the right.
Draw lines to match the pairs of antonyms.
Then color the pictures.

sick

little

open

night

big

day

well

closed

Skills: Recognizing antonyms; Vocabulary development

ANTONYMS

Antonyms are words that are opposites.
Look at the pictures and words on the left.
Look at the words and pictures on the right.
Draw lines to match the pairs of antonyms.
Then color the pictures.

sit

sink

tall

in

out

short

stand

float

Skills: Recognizing antonyms; Vocabulary development

ANTONYMS

Antonyms are words that are opposites.
Look at the pictures and words on the left.
Look at the words and pictures on the right.
Draw lines to match the pairs of antonyms.
Then color the pictures.

strong

up

new

top

down

old

weak

bottom

Skills: Recognizing antonyms; Vocabulary development

ANTONYMS

Antonyms are words that are opposites.
Look at the picture and word in each box.
Look at the words at the top of the page.
Write a word from the top box that is the opposite of the word in each box.

weak   cold   empty   up

full

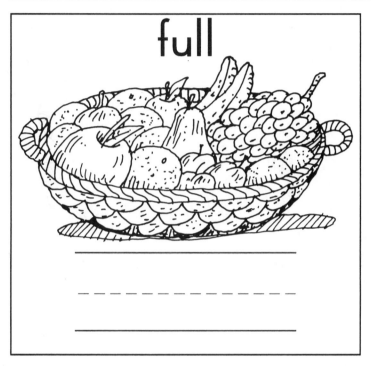

_____

_ _ _ _ _ _ _ _ _ _

_____

hot

_____

_ _ _ _ _ _ _ _ _ _

_____

strong

_____

_ _ _ _ _ _ _ _ _ _

_____

down

_____

_ _ _ _ _ _ _ _ _ _

_____

Skills: Identifying antonyms; Vocabulary development

ANTONYMS

Antonyms are words that are opposites.
Look at the picture and word in each box.
Look at the words at the top of the page.
Write a word from the top box that is the opposite of the word in each box.

open	day	small	front

back

_____

- - - - - - - -

_____

night

_____

- - - - - - - -

_____

large

_____

- - - - - - - -

_____

closed

_____

- - - - - - - -

_____

Skills: Identifying antonyms; Vocabulary development

ANTONYMS

Antonyms are words that are opposites.
Look at the picture and word in each box.
Look at the words at the top of the page.
Write a word from the top box that is the opposite of the word in each box.

| hard | dry | stand | young |

wet

_____

- - - - - - - - - - - -

_____

old

_____

- - - - - - - - - - - -

_____

sit

_____

- - - - - - - - - - - -

_____

soft

_____

- - - - - - - - - - - -

_____

Skills: Identifying antonyms; Vocabulary development

283

ANTONYMS

Antonyms are words that are opposites.
Look at the picture and word in each box.
Look at the words at the top of the page.
Write a word from the top box that is the opposite of the word in each box.

awake	happy	bottom	out

in

_____

_____

sad

_____

_____

top

_____

_____

asleep

_____

_____

Skills: Identifying antonyms; Vocabulary development

284

ANTONYMS

Antonyms are words that are opposites.
Look at the picture and word in each box.
Look at the words at the top of the page.
Write a word from the top box that is the opposite of the word in each box.

well	short	float	smile

frown

HUMPF!

_____

— — — — — — — — — —

_____

sick

_____

— — — — — — — — — —

_____

tall

_____

— — — — — — — — — —

_____

sink

_____

— — — — — — — — — —

_____

Skills: Identifying antonyms; Vocabulary development

ANTONYMS

Antonyms are words that are opposites.
Look at the words in each castle.
Circle the words in each castle that are antonyms.

fat
cold
sad
thin

noisy
quiet
funny
happy

open
bad
good
dirty

baby
puppy
slow
fast

Skills: Identifying antonyms; Vocabulary development; Recognizing antonyms in a group of words

ANTONYMS

Antonyms are words that are opposites.
Look at the words in each balloon.
Circle the words in each balloon that are antonyms.

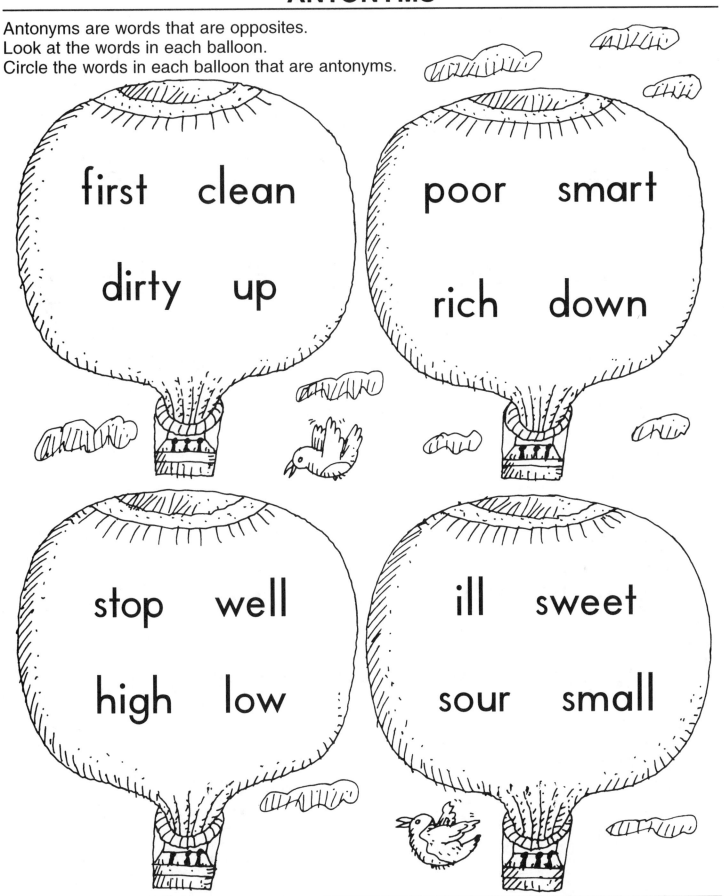

first   clean

dirty   up

poor   smart

rich   down

stop   well

high   low

ill   sweet

sour   small

Skills: Identifying antonyms; Vocabulary development; Recognizing antonyms in a group of words

ANTONYMS

Antonyms are words that are opposites.
Look at the words in each flower.
Circle the words in each flower that are antonyms.

stop   go
fast   quiet

shut   glad
open   loud

good   thin
strong   weak

quiet   top
bottom   large

Skills: Identifying antonyms; Vocabulary development; Recognizing antonyms in a group of words

ANTONYMS

Antonyms are words that are opposites.
Look at the words in each shell.
Circle the words in each shell that are antonyms.

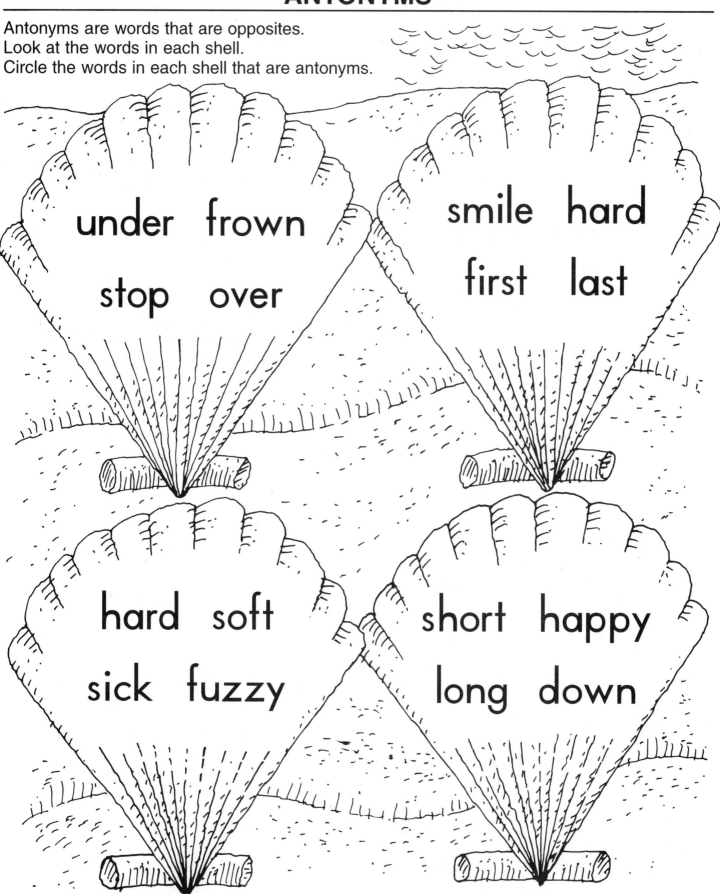

under   frown
stop   over

smile   hard
first   last

hard   soft
sick   fuzzy

short   happy
long   down

Skills: Identifying antonyms; Vocabulary development; Recognizing antonyms in a group of words

ANTONYMS

Antonyms are words that are opposites.
Look at the words in each cake.
Circle the words in each cake that are antonyms.

messy

neat   sweet

small

ugly

slow   first

pretty

light

sour   dark

noisy

low

new   high

slow

HOMONYMS

Homonyms are words that sound the same but have different spellings and meanings.
Look at the word in each mitten.
Look at the words in the box at the top of the page.
Find a word from the box that sounds the same as the word in each mitten.
Write it in the other mitten.

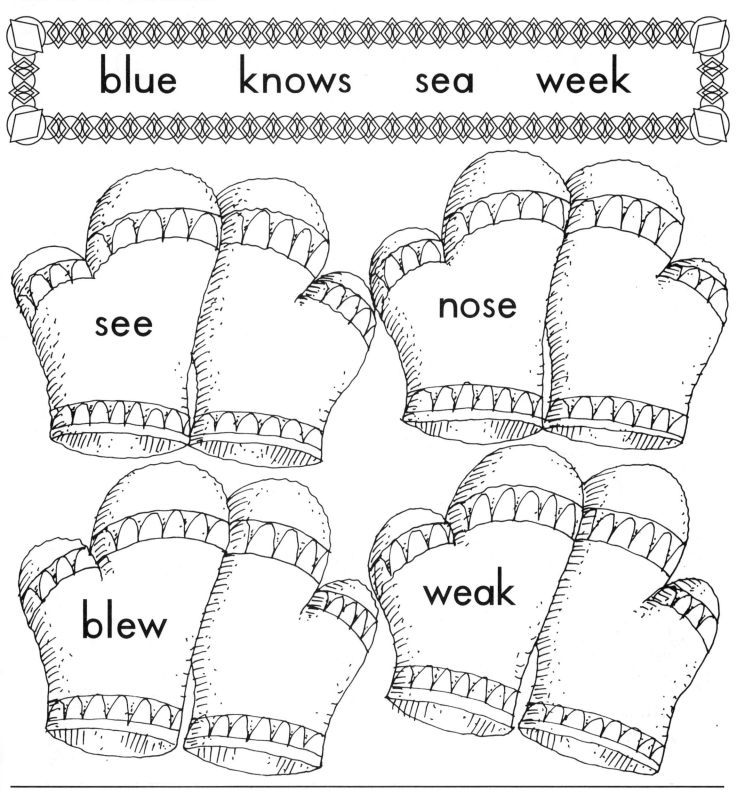

blue   knows   sea   week

see

nose

blew

weak

Skills: Identifying homonyms; Vocabulary development

HOMONYMS

Homonyms are words that sound the same but have different spellings and meanings.
Look at the word in each shoe.
Look at the words in the box at the top of the page.
Find a word from the box that sounds the same as the word in each shoe.
Write it in the other shoe.

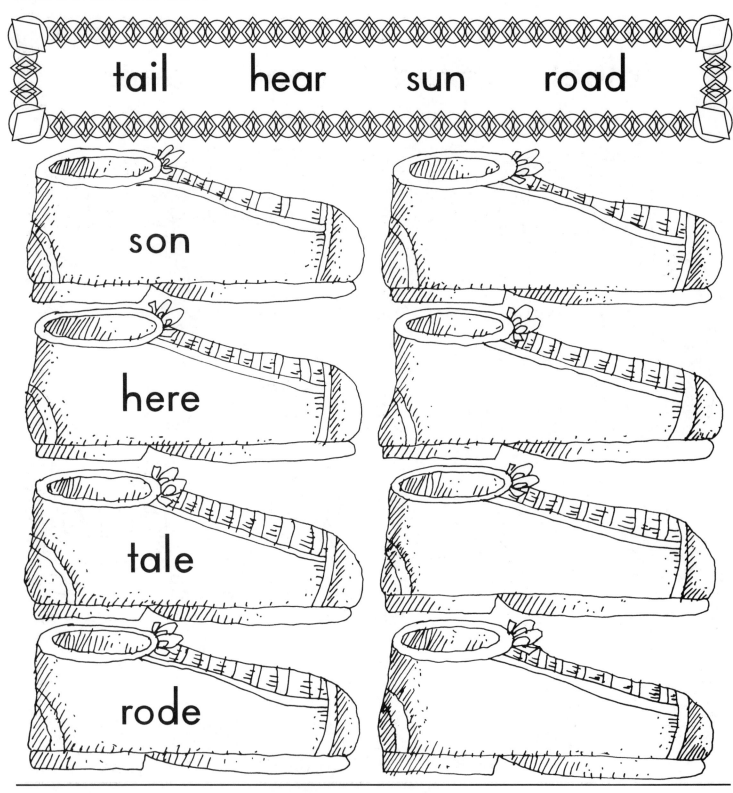

tail   hear   sun   road

son

here

tale

rode

Skills: Identifying homonyms; Vocabulary development

HOMONYMS

Homonyms are words that sound the same but have different spellings and meanings.
Look at the word in each sock.
Look at the words in the box at the top of the page.
Find a word from the box that sounds the same as the word in each sock.
Write it in the other sock.

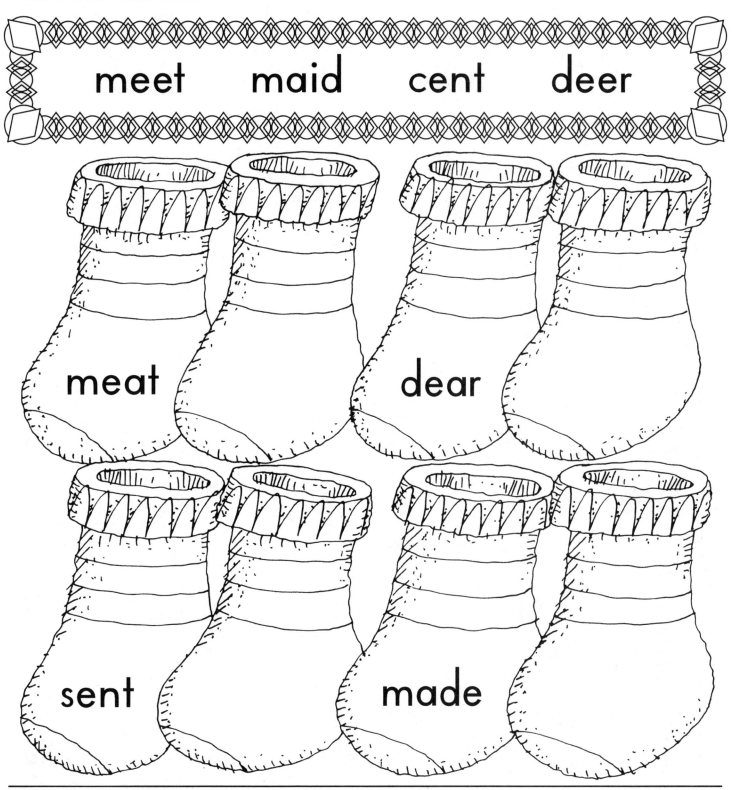

meet   maid   cent   deer

meat

dear

sent

made

HOMONYMS

Homonyms are words that sound the same but have different spellings and meanings.
Look at the word in each snowman.
Look at the words in the box at the top of the page.
Find a word from the box that sounds the same as the word in each snowman.
Write it in the other part of the snowman.

sail   pain   pail   heel

heal

pane

sale

pale

Skills: Identifying homonyms; Vocabulary development

294

HOMONYMS

Homonyms are words that sound the same but have different spellings and meanings.
Look at the word in each book.
Look at the words in the box at the top of the page.
Find a word from the box that sounds the same as the word in each book.
Write it on the other page of the book.

beet   to   not   our

two

knot

hour

beat

Skills: Identifying homonyms; Vocabulary development

HOMONYMS

Homonyms are words that sound the same but have different spellings and meanings.
Look at the pictures below.
Look at the pair of words beside each picture.
Circle the word that goes with the picture.

too
two

night
knight

dear
deer

son
sun

Skills: Identifying homonyms; Vocabulary development; Distinguishing between homonyms

HOMONYMS

Homonyms are words that sound the same but have different spellings and meanings.
Look at the pictures below.
Look at the pair of words beside each picture.
Circle the word that goes with the picture.

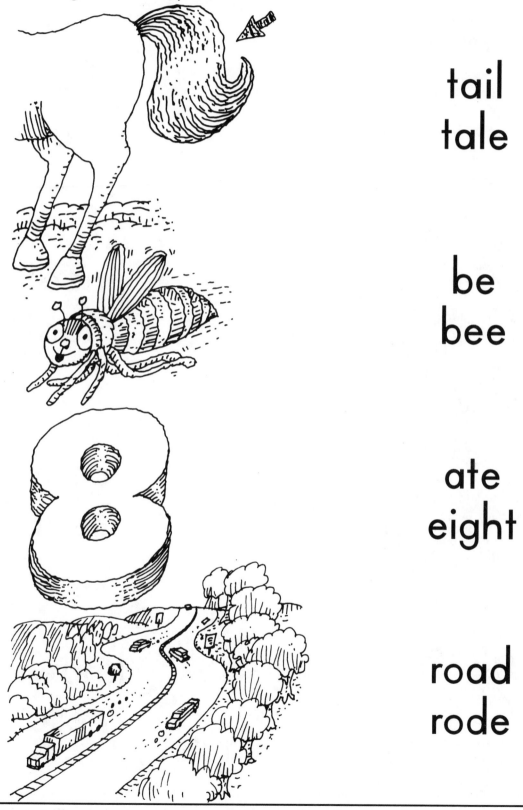

tail
tale

be
bee

ate
eight

road
rode

Skills: Identifying homonyms; Vocabulary development; Distinguishing between homonyms

HOMONYMS

Homonyms are words that sound the same but have different spellings and meanings.
Look at the pictures below.
Look at the pair of words beside each picture.
Circle the word that goes with the picture.

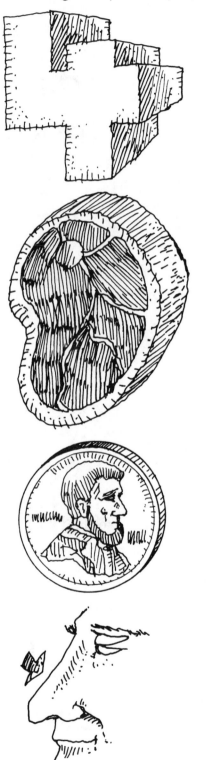

for
four

meet
meat

cent
sent

knows
nose

Skills: Identifying homonyms; Vocabulary development; Distinguishing between homonyms

HOMONYMS

Homonyms are words that sound the same but have different spellings and meanings.
Look at the pictures below.
Look at the pair of words beside each picture.
Circle the word that goes with the picture.

pair
pear

ant
aunt

bare
bear

see
sea

Skills: Identifying homonyms; Vocabulary development; Distinguishing between homonyms

HOMONYMS

Homonyms are words that sound the same but have different spellings and meanings.
Look at the pictures below.
Look at the pair of words beside each picture.
Circle the word that goes with the picture.

so
sew

hair
hare

I
eye

four
for

Skills: Identifying homonyms; Vocabulary development; Distinguishing between homonyms

HOMONYMS

Homonyms are words that sound the same but have different spellings and meanings.
Look at the sentences below.
Circle the two words that are homonyms in each sentence.

I put on an eye patch.

Pat ate eight cherries.

We rode our bikes on the road.

I see the boats in the sea.

Skills: Identifying homonyms; Vocabulary development; Recognizing homonyms in a group of words

HOMONYMS

Homonyms are words that sound the same but have different spellings and meanings.
Look at the sentences below.
Circle the two words that are homonyms in each sentence.

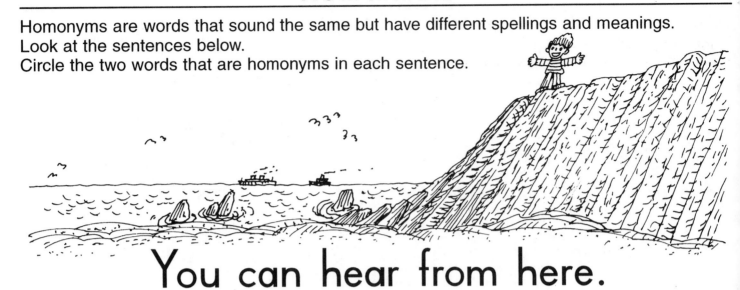

You can hear from here.

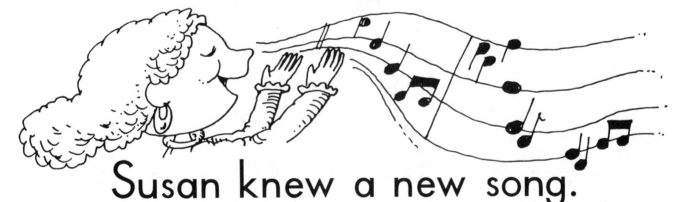

We want a table for four.

Susan knew a new song.

Tell the tale of the cat's tail.

Skills: Identifying homonyms; Vocabulary development; Recognizing homonyms in a group of words

HOMONYMS

Homonyms are words that sound the same but have different spellings and meanings.
Look at the sentences below.
Circle the two words that are homonyms in each sentence.

He blew up a blue balloon.

The maid made our beds.

Meet me at the meat counter.

Give two presents to him.

Skills: Identifying homonyms; Vocabulary development; Recognizing homonyms in a group of words

HOMONYMS

Homonyms are words that sound the same but have different spellings and meanings.
Look at the sentences below.
Circle the two words that are homonyms in each sentence.

My son sat in the sun.

Do not undo the knot.

He felt weak all week.

My dear, look at the deer.

Skills: Identifying homonyms; Vocabulary development; Recognizing homonyms in a group of words

HOMONYMS

Homonyms are words that sound the same but have different spellings and meanings.
Look at the sentences below.
Circle the two words that are homonyms in each sentence.

My sore heel will soon heal.

A pair of twins share a pear.

So few people can sew.

I said hi in a high voice.

Skills: Identifying homonyms; Vocabulary development; Recognizing homonyms in a group of words

COMPOUND WORDS

Compound words are made up of two words put together.
Look at the pictures and the two words underneath.
Put the words together to make a compound word.
Write that word on the line.

_____

- - - - - - - - - - - - - - - - - - - -

_____

_____

- - - - - - - - - - - - - - - - - - - -

_____

_____

- - - - - - - - - - - - - - - - - - - -

_____

_____

- - - - - - - - - - - - - - - - - - - -

_____

Skills: Identification of compound words; Vocabulary development; Making compound words from two words

306

COMPOUND WORDS

Compound words are made up of two words put together.
Look at the pictures and the two words underneath.
Put the words together to make a compound word.
Write that word on the line.

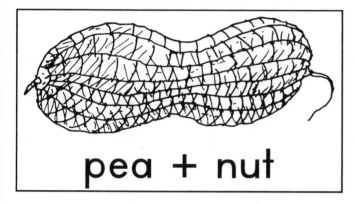

pea + nut

_____

- - - - - - - - - - - - - - - - -

_____

cup + cake

_____

- - - - - - - - - - - - - - - - -

_____

tea + cup

_____

- - - - - - - - - - - - - - - - -

_____

wheel + chair

_____

- - - - - - - - - - - - - - - - -

_____

Skills: Identification of compound words; Vocabulary development; Making compound words from two words

COMPOUND WORDS

Compound words are made up of two words put together.
Look at the pictures and the two words underneath.
Put the words together to make a compound word.
Write that word on the line.

tooth + paste

_____

- - - - - - - - - - - - - - - - - -

_____

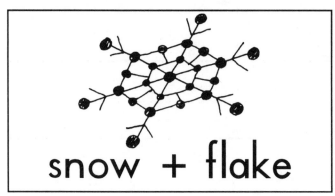

snow + flake

_____

- - - - - - - - - - - - - - - - - -

_____

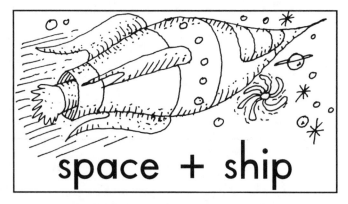

space + ship

_____

- - - - - - - - - - - - - - - - - -

_____

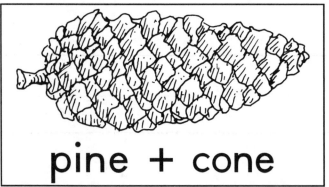

pine + cone

_____

- - - - - - - - - - - - - - - - - -

_____

Skills: Identification of compound words; Vocabulary development; Making compound words from two words

COMPOUND WORDS

Compound words are made up of two words put together.
Look at the pictures and the two words underneath.
Put the words together to make a compound word.
Write that word on the line.

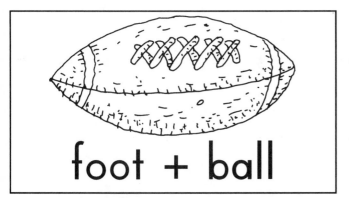

foot + ball

_____

- - - - - - - - - - -

_____

black + bird

_____

- - - - - - - - - - -

_____

gold + fish

_____

- - - - - - - - - - -

_____

butter + fly

_____

- - - - - - - - - - -

_____

Skills: Identification of compound words; Vocabulary development; Making compound words from two words

COMPOUND WORDS

Compound words are made up of two words put together.
Look at the pictures and the two words underneath.
Put the words together to make a compound word.
Write that word on the line.

bath + tub

_____

- - - - - - - - - - - - -

_____

rain + coat

_____

- - - - - - - - - - - - -

_____

row + boat

_____

- - - - - - - - - - - - -

_____

air + plane

_____

- - - - - - - - - - - - -

_____

Skills: Identification of compound words; Vocabulary development; Making compound words from two words

COMPOUND WORDS

Compound words are made up of two words put together.
Look at the words in each box.
Put the two words together to make a compound word.
Then draw a picture to go with that word.

candle stick	hive bee
------------------------------	------------------------------

fire place	brush hair
------------------------------	------------------------------

Skills: Understanding compound words; Vocabulary development; Making compound words from two words

COMPOUND WORDS

Compound words are made up of two words put together.
Look at the words in each box.
Put the two words together to make a compound word.
Then draw a picture to go with that word.

house dog	book mark

fly fire	fish gold

Skills: Understanding compound words; Vocabulary development; Making compound words from two words

COMPOUND WORDS

Compound words are made up of two words put together.
Look at the words in each box.
Put the two words together to make a compound word.
Then draw a picture to go with that word.

glasses eye	rail road
snow suit	flower sun

Skills: Understanding compound words; Vocabulary development; Making compound words from two words

COMPOUND WORDS

Compound words are made up of two words put together.
Look at the words in each box.
Put the two words together to make a compound word.
Then draw a picture to go with that word.

pop corn	pot tea

ball snow	hand shake

Skills: Understanding compound words; Vocabulary development; Making compound words from two words

314

COMPOUND WORDS

Compound words are made up of two words put together.
Look at the words in each box.
Put the two words together to make a compound word.
Then draw a picture to go with that word.

key hole	cycle motor
night gown	book note

Skills: Understanding compound words; Vocabulary development; Making compound words from two words

COMPOUND WORDS

Compound words are made up of two words put together.
Look at the pictures and words in the box.
Read the sentences below them.
Complete each sentence with a compound word from the box.
Then color the pictures.

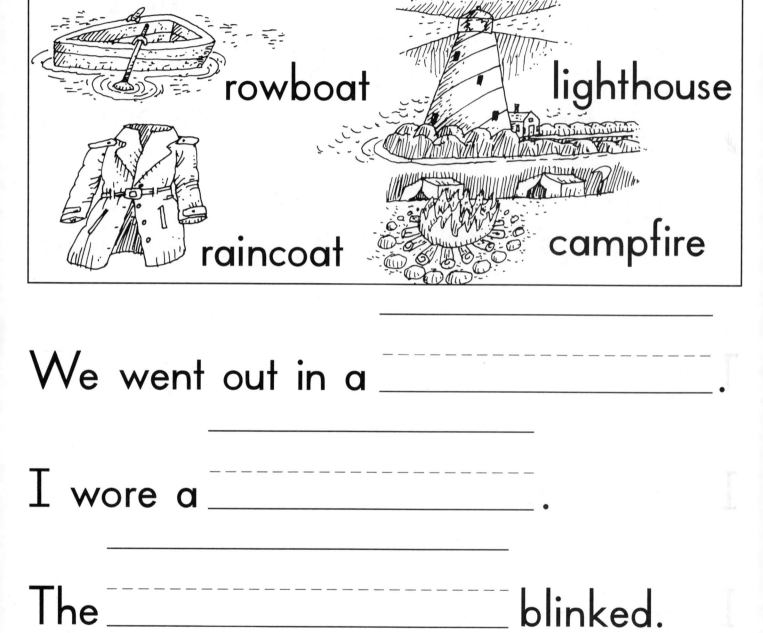

rowboat

lighthouse

raincoat

campfire

We went out in a _____.

I wore a _____.

The _____ blinked.

A _____ burned on shore.

Skills: Understanding compound words; Vocabulary development; Using compound words in sentences

COMPOUND WORDS

Compound words are made up of two words put together.
Look at the pictures and words in the box.
Read the sentences below them.
Complete each sentence with a compound word from the box.
Then color the pictures.

staircase

bedroom

doorbell

grandmother

The _____ rang twice.

I was in the _____ .

I ran down the _____ .

My _____ came in.

Skills: Understanding compound words; Vocabulary development; Using compound words in sentences

COMPOUND WORDS

Compound words are made up of two words put together.
Look at the pictures and words in the box.
Read the sentences below them.
Complete each sentence with a compound word from the box.
Then color the pictures.

cupcake

drumstick

cornbread

corncob

I ate a _____ for dinner.

Mom baked _____.

I left the _____ on my plate.

I had a _____ for dessert.

Skills: Understanding compound words; Vocabulary development; Using compound words in sentences

COMPOUND WORDS

Compound words are made up of two words put together.
Look at the pictures and words in the box.
Read the sentences below them.
Complete each sentence with a compound word from the box.
Then color the pictures.

hilltop

cowboy

sunset

rainbow

The _____ rode his horse.

He stopped on a _____.

He saw a _____.

He watched the _____.

Skills: Understanding compound words; Vocabulary development; Using compound words in sentences

COMPOUND WORDS

Compound words are made up of two words put together.
Look at the pictures and words in the box.
Read the sentences below them.
Complete each sentence with a compound word from the box.
Then color the pictures.

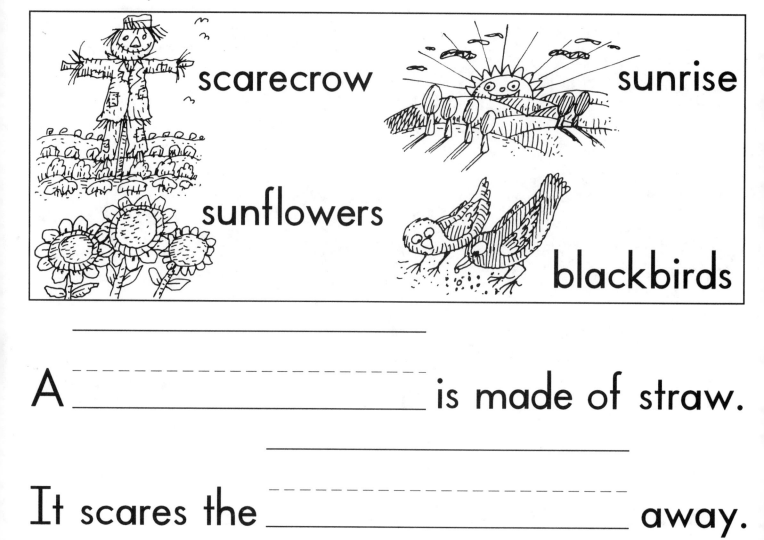

scarecrow

sunrise

sunflowers

blackbirds

A _____ is made of straw.

It scares the _____ away.

The farmer is up at _____.

He grows tall _____.

Skills: Understanding compound words; Vocabulary development; Using compound words in sentences